Essential Fashion Illustration:
Digital

Loreto Binvignat Streeter

BEVERLY MASSACHUSETTS

ROCKPORT
PUBLISHERS

Copyright © 2010 by **maomao** publications
First published in 2010 in the United States of America by
Rockport Publishers, a member of
Quayside Publishing Group
100 Cummings Center
Suite 406-L
Beverly, MA 01915-6101
Telephone: (978) 282-9590
Fax: (978) 283-2742
www.rockpub.com

ISBN-13: 978-1-59253-632-0
ISBN-10: 1-59253-632-8

10 9 8 7 6 5 4 3 2 1

Publisher: Paco Asensio
Editorial coordination: Anja Llorella Oriol
Concepts, illustrations, and texts: Loreto Binvignat Streeter
Text edition: Macarena San Martín
Art director: Emma Termes Parera
Layout: Maira Purman
English translation: Cillero & de Motta

Editorial project:
maomao publications
Via Laietana, 32, 4th fl., of. 104
08003 Barcelona, Spain
Tel. : +34 93 268 80 88
Fax : +34 93 317 42 08
www.maomaopublications.com

Printed in Singapore

CONTENTS

6 INTRODUCTION
8 Equipment
10 Photoshop
13 Illustrator
16 How to clean a
    scanned image
20 How to scan different
    parts of an image
24 Photographic camera

28 LINES
28 Basic vector lines
32 Creative brush
36 Live trace
40 Line color
42 Black lines
46 Creative lines
50 Stamp filter

54 COLOR
54 Coloring with Photoshop
58 Coloring with Illustrator
62 Color retouching
66 Color grading in Illustrator
70 Color grading in Photoshop

74 TRANSPARENCY
74 Transparency in Photoshop
76 Multiply mode
80 Creative transparency
86 Composition

92 PATTERNED FABRIC
92 Basic patterned fabrics
    with Photoshop

96 Creative digital patterned fabric
100 Adjusting the patterned
     fabric in Photoshop
104 Basic patterned fabrics
     with Illustrator
108 Patterned fabric with
     Illustrator and Photoshop
112 Creative patterns with Photoshop
116 Patterns with symbols

120 TEXTURES
120 Color halftone filter
124 Texture with fonts
128 Textured background
132 Vintage texture

136 COLLAGE
136 Basic digital collage
140 Vintage creative collage
144 Contemporary creative collage

148 DIGITAL PAINTING
148 Painting with Photoshop
154 Tracing with Photoshop
158 Illustration and photographs
162 Tracing with Illustrator

168 MIXED TECHNIQUES
168 Watercolor
172 Working with splotches
176 Drawing and photographs
180 Vector drawing and photographs
184 Pencil and wood texture
188 Pencil and photographs

INTRODUCTION

Fashion illustration is an essential tool in the world of fashion design. It enables pieces to be represented and the designer's main ideas of a certain concept or look to be conveyed.

The first fashion illustrations appeared some 500 years ago. They were predominant in fashion magazines until the early twentieth century. At that time, howver, advances in printing led to the inclusion of photographs in magazines, which replaced illustration, particularly in the most important publications of the day, such as *Vogue* and *Harper's Bazaar*. But because photography is a faithful representation of reality, and illustration is an artistic representation, with more space for imagination and subjectivity, illustration was never completely lost. There were always people interested in showing their particular view of fashion.

In recent years, digital technology has breathed new life into illustration in general. Among other things, it enables techniques to be combined and has brought a speed to illustration tasks that was previously unknown, producing results that were unheard of before. This revival has also spread to fashion illustration. Digital illustration is increasingly being used in publishing and advertising, to represent designs and promote designers, labels, and stores, and as it does, it pushes the boundaries of fashion.

The pages of this book feature step-by-step instructions for creating digital illustration at the hand of fashion illustrator and designer Loreto Binvignat Streeter. The book begins with her explanation of the basics of working with digital technology — for example, cleaning an image and digitally retouching it, or tracing a figure with vectors — and gradually shows you new techniques and styles that she applies in each exercise. You are not required to be an expert with Photoshop and Illustrator software to follow them. You only need to be a little familiar with them. If you do all of the exercises in this book, in a few days you will be able to create digital illustrations with a certain level of complexity and creativity, and decide for yourself what methods and tools suit you best when you continue to illustrate.

The illustrations included here can be classified into one of two groups: basic or creative. Basic illustrations are those that a designer would use to bring designs to life, for the purpose of representing garments and pieces as closely as possible to real life for clients and buyers to see the presented designs clearly. On the contrary, creative illustrations mostly resemble those that a fashion illustrator would not use to give a realistic impression of a piece or a collection, but rather use to transmit the essence or main idea.

EQUIPMENT

Here is a description of the equipment needed for creating digital illustrations. Added to this are the materials normally used for illustration on paper.

It is advisable to buy quality items but at reasonable cost. There is no need to go all out and have the latest and best in brands and quality. All you need is something to make digital illustrations with; in the end, what gives quality to the illustration is the care you give to it and the effort and creativity that go into making it.

COMPUTER
This can be a PC or a Mac. It is important to have enough RAM to run the required programs (2 GB are enough for the computer to work at its best). It is recommended a minimum of 300 GB of memory in the hard drive.

EXTERNAL HARD DRIVE
This is useful for backing up the information you have in your computer and, obviously, to have more available storage memory space. Digital artists need one, given that they are constantly creating high-definition files and using programs that take up a lot of memory. Having a hard drive of this kind enables your computer to work better. They are not expensive compared to the benefits they provide, and they are available in fixed (directly connected to a power supply) and portable formats.

USB FLASH DRIVE
Having one of these is essential because you will constantly be copying files from one computer to another. The possibility of importing and exporting files with one infinitely makes it extremely useful. It should have at least 2 GB of memory.

GRAPHICS TABLET

This is of great use because it is much more precise than a mouse. It might seem a little difficult to use at first because of its sensitivity, but you can adjust it to suit your style. The advantage of the tablet is that it enables you to draw digitally as if you were doing so with a pencil or paintbrush and to use digital programs and their tools with greater ease and precision. What size tablet to acquire depends on the precision needed for the job – a larger one gives higher resolution, but a small one can be perfect for working with – or how much money you want to spend, although graphics tablets are generally available at a reasonable price.

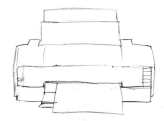

PRINTER

This is a support to the creative process that lets you print out drafts of your work. Unless you have a professional-quality printer at home or in the studio, it is better to have final illustrations printed professionally because the quality offered is far better than that achieved with a basic printer.

SCANNER

Your scanner should at least be A4 size, although the bigger the better. The scanners on the market are generally good; a good quality device can be acquired at a reasonable price and can serve all of your requirements, unless you have something very specific in mind.

DIGITAL CAMERA

If you use a camera as the way to digitize your illustrations before working with them on the computer, you will need to have a good quality one. If this is not the case, it is highly likely that you will have to do some major retouching to your images in Photoshop and that the resolution will not be the best. If working with an average priced camera, you will have to take your photographs with the greatest precision possible and at the highest resolution if you are to make working with them easier.

PHOTOSHOP

Here is a general overview of the features and uses of this program. As there is a wide range of possibilities with this program, this explanation will focus on those most commonly used in fashion illustration, which are image editing and correction, and digital color application. If you have a specific question about its use at any time, the best thing to do is use the Help menu to find the solution to your problem.

Photoshop software works like a painting and photography studio. You work over a digital canvas that serves for editing images, retouching photos, and digital coloring. When you use this program, you work with a bitmap, which means that every image you handle is composed of pixels.

A pixel is the smallest unit of a graphic image and is generally represented as a square. The number of pixels an image has determines its quality or resolution, to use digital speak. For illustration – and for all images that are to be printed – the working resolution is 300 dpi (dots per inch), meaning that there are 300 pixels along a line measuring one inch, while the screen resolution – images that will not be printed but only used on the computer – is 72 dpi. These images show the difference in resolution between an image at 300 dpi (left) and another at 72 dpi (right).

Command menu

Context options

Tools

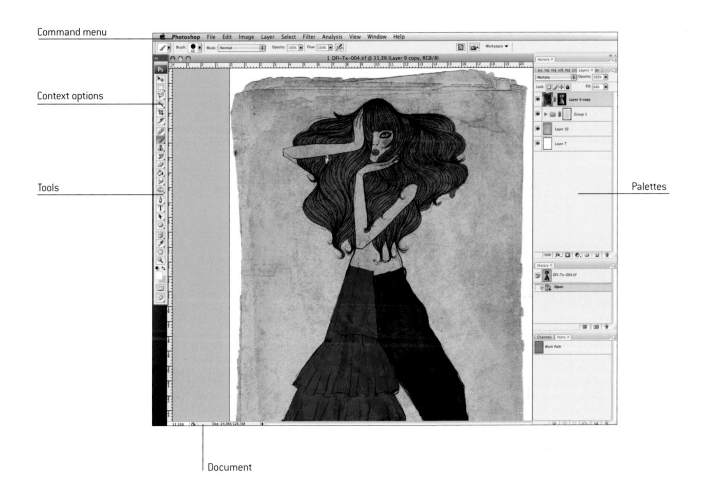

Palettes

Document

The main features of the Photoshop interface are:

COMMAND MENU
The menu bar organizes the different commands into groups: File, Edit, Image, Layer, Select, Filter, Analysis, View, Window, and Help.

CONTEXT OPTIONS
This bar shows the different options available for the tool you have selected.

TOOLS
This bar contains the necessary tools for working with the software. Those related by function are grouped together.

PALETTES
These are windows that help to control and view the work being done. They can be placed anywhere on the workspace and the ones you want to be visible can be selected in the Window menu. The example shows the Layers, History, and Paths palettes.

DOCUMENT
This shows the image being worked on. A number of different document windows can be kept open at the same time.

These are some of the most commonly used objects and commands for retouching images.

TOOLBAR

This is very important for creating and modifying images. The following are the most commonly used: Move, Rectangular Marquee, Lasso, Magic Wand, Crop, Correction Brush, Brush, Clone Stamp, Eraser, Paint Bucket, Dodge, Pen, Horizontal Text, Path Selection, Custom Shape, Eyedropper, Hand, Zoom, and Foreground/Background Color.

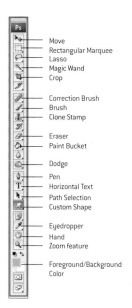

BRUSH

When the Brush tool is selected, this panel pops up at the top, below the Photoshop menu (in this example, where the brush appears with the 30), showing the current brush settings (type, master diameter, and tip hardness) and their context options. This is a very important panel as it is used continuously in the exercises. It offers a choice from a wide variety of brushes, which can be modified with these options. Flow is a very useful brush option because it enables the intensity of paint application to be regulated.

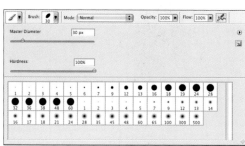

ADJUSTMENTS

These are used directly to retouch and correct the main properties of images such as color, hue, saturation, and contrast. The adjustments are found on the Image menu (Image>Adjustments) and can be applied directly over the image, or what is more recommendable, over an Adjustment Layer, which is a duplicate of the layer the image is located on, so that modifications are only made on this layer, with the original being preserved.

FILTERS

These are quite common in this program, although they are used on only few occasions for the type of exercises carried out in this book. Filters let you create a host of effects – they can even be added to others – and can be applied to whole layers or selected areas.

ILLUSTRATOR

This program works like an art workshop. It is based on vectors that are used to create digital drawings; although it also lets you edit and retouch bitmap images to a certain point. This is a very extensive and complex program, meaning that mastering it requires a great deal of time and patience. In order to use it confidently, at least the most basic points need to be learned. The exercises given in this book only require the basic tools for making vector outlines and pictures. One of the great advantages of working in this way (with vectors), unlike working with Photoshop, is that everything that you draw or color can be enlarged without losing resolution, as shown here:

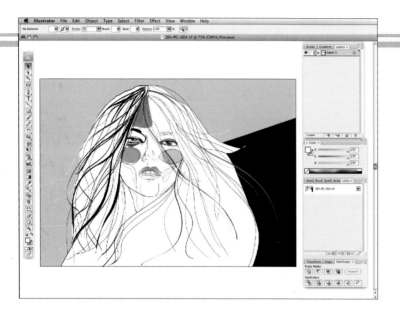

Given that Photoshop and Illustrator are from the same company (Adobe), the workspace is practically the same. They also have common main components in the command menu, the tools with their respective options, the palettes, and the document.

It works in a similar way to Photoshop:

TOOLBAR
There are many tools that are identical to Photoshop, and they are also grouped according to function. The most commonly used tools are Selection, Direct Selection, Magic Wand, Lasso, Pen, Type, Line, Rectangle, Brush, Rotate, Symbol Sprayer, Gradient Mesh, Gradient, Eyedropper, Crop Area, Eraser, Hand, Zoom, Swap Fill/Stroke Colors, and Gradient/Color/Line. Of these, the tool you will use most is the Pen, the basic implement for creating vector outlines.

PALETTES
The picture again shows the Layers palette. Illustrator also works with layers. This option helps to organize the drawing, but, unlike Photoshop, layers are not always necessary. Color, Links and Pathfinder palettes are also shown. The last of these is very useful as it lets you create shapes from overlapping figures.

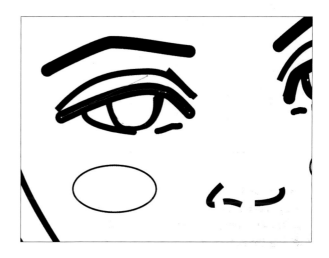

TRACING VECTORS

Vector shapes are created as a set of dots. Controlling these dots when drawing can be a little difficult so it is necessary to practice and gain experience in handling them, particularly all of their direction lines, which determine the curve of the outlines depending on their length and how pronounced they are. The fewer points there are on a curve, the cleaner the line.

HOW TO CLEAN A SCANNED IMAGE

When working with digital illustration, you should first make a freehand drawing or draft to work on using the computer. This exercise shows how to clean a draft or drawing using Photoshop.

Before scanning a drawing, you should make sure it is as finished as possible. If the drawing is done well at the start, the result will be good. However, if the base is not right, it will be more difficult and laborious to fix it digitally. Few changes should be made to the base drawing, which is why you should try to use as few lines as possible – cleaning will be easier and faster before beginning the digital part.

The resolution the drawing is scanned at will determine the size and weight of the resulting file; if it is very large, it may be difficult to work with if your computer does not have enough RAM. It is important to know the purpose of each image being scanned. To obtain a digitized image at a good resolution, it should be scanned at 300 dpi as a TIFF file. Where work will be done in sections, a resolution of 150 dpi can be used, whereas for high-resolution projects and some black and white images, scanning can be at up to 600 dpi.

To scan this drawing, a TIFF file of 300 dpi was made in grayscale, considering it is a pencil drawing.

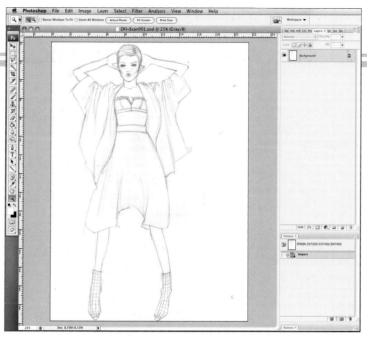

1. Never work on the original. Make a copy of the layer where the image is located and work on the copy. This way you can do all kinds of experiments, and there will no problem if they turn out wrong because the original will still be intact.

2. You generally start by adjusting the levels (Image>Adjustments>Levels). You can alter the intensity of the blacks, grays, and whites by moving the arrows. It can also be adjusted numerically or with the eyedropper.

3. When the desired line is achieved and the background has been cleaned enough, use the Polygonal Lasso and follow the outline of the figure (you can also use the simple Lasso, although as the Polygonal one lets you mark the dots, it makes the job easier).

4. When the figure is closed, choose Select>Invert (Ctrl+Shift+I) to switch to the background. By doing this, you can crop the image leaving the white of the lower layer (if you have not already added a white layer, you can do this now).

5. Once the background is removed, you have to clean the edges of the figure. Use the eraser for this. You will have to change the size of the image depending on the area you are cleaning.

6. You can also choose specific areas with the Rectangular Marquee or Magnetic Lasso tools and so modify the levels of these areas only.

7. You have to make sure that every part – including the spaces between the arms, for instance – are completely clean and that the background is truly white.

8. With a clean background, you can intensify the line by duplicating the image (layer). Select Multiply in merge layer mode.

9. This action turns the white transparent, leaving the line twice as intense as before. To soften a little, adjust the fill and opacity of the layer.

HOW TO SCAN DIFFERENT PARTS OF AN IMAGE

Often you will need to work with images that are larger than the scanner, but this does not mean they cannot be digitized. This exercise shows you how to scan the parts of an image and later join them in Photoshop.

1. Place the paper on the scanner so that the edges are lined up perfectly with it from the corner of the sheet. In this way, all of the sections to be scanned will have the same angle and can be joined without gaps.

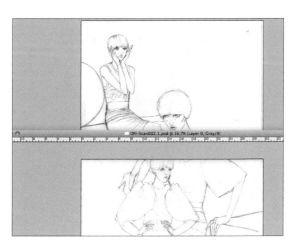

2. The drawing has been scanned in two parts, both at 300 dpi as TIFF files and in grayscale, meaning that there are now two document files.

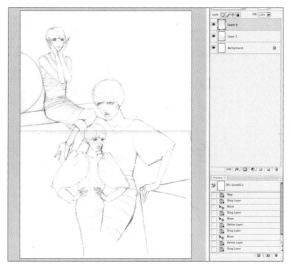

3. Open a new document in Photoshop with the dimensions of the original image and a resolution of 300 dpi, the same as the scanned images. Copy the two scanned files and paste them onto the new document (you can also click and drag them) and arrange them like the original.

4. To make the images coincide, the best thing is to add a layer in Multiply mode (on the dropdown menu next to Opacity and Fill in the Layers palette). Enlarge the image so that the overlapping lines can be seen in detail.

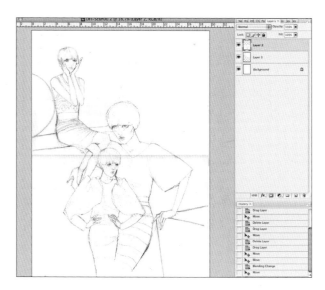

5. When the image has been fitted together, set the layer to Normal. On doing this, a darker band will appear caused by the curving of the paper during scanning.

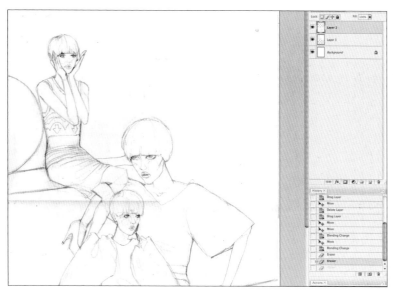

6. Use the eraser to remove the band. As one part of the image has been superimposed over the other, you can erase this area from one layer without erasing the drawing.

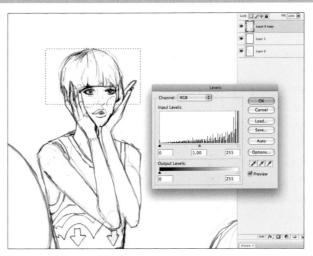

7. Join the layers together (Layer>Merge Down or Ctrl+E) to produce a single image. You can now clean it and adjust its levels.

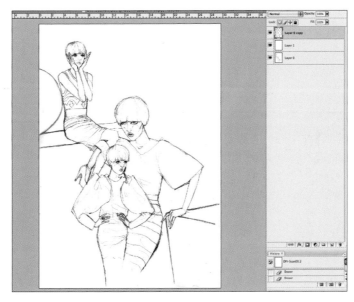

8. The image is now ready to be digitally modified as you wish.

PHOTOGRAPHIC CAMERA

A digital camera is used to digitize large-scale images or those on a support that makes scanning impossible. For the best results, it is recommended that a camera with the highest resolution available be used, and always with a tripod. The photo should be taken in natural light – so as not to alter the colors of the image – and as fully front on as possible, so as not to create odd perspectives.

1. When photographing an image, it is best to leave a margin and not to square the photo completely as this can be done easily in Photoshop.

2. Once the image has been imported into the computer, open it in Photoshop and use the Crop tool to remove as much of the margin as possible.

3. It is very difficult to take a fully front-on photograph, which means that there is always a small distortion and the edges will not line up completely with the document. Sometimes the Crop tool is not enough.

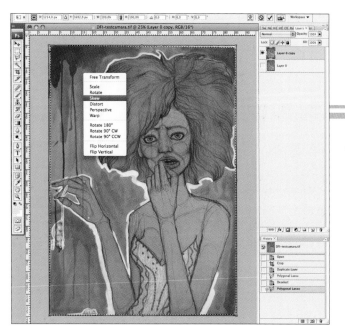

4. To square the image, select the area with the Polygonal Lasso. Select Free Transform (Edit menu or Ctrl+T), and by right clicking over the area with the mouse (using Click+Ctrl for Mac) choose the Skew option. This adjusts the edges of the selected area with the corners of the document.

5. The next step is to retouch the image. Start with the levels, but instead of using the Adjustment menu, look for a half-white and half-black circle in the Layers palette. This enables you to create an Adjustment Layer. There are a number of different options, Levels among them.

6. The advantage of working with these layers is that if they are erased or become invisible, the adjustment disappears. It is also good to use Color Balance to recover the original colors.

7. The third Adjustment Layer to be created is Black and White, which removes the color and lets you work easily with the black drawing line.

This layer is created in Multiply mode and the values are adjusted for the fill so as to highlight the line, but without saturating it.

8. The image is ready for working with. As it is still with the Adjustment Layers, select Layer>Flatten Image in the menu to leave a single image, although this is not necessary.

LINES // BASIC VECTOR LINES

After the explanation of how to transform the lines in a freehand drawing, it is now time to show you how to draw lines using vectors in Illustrator.

This is the most commonly used digital line, and Illustrator is the most suitable program for this kind of exercise.

Although this is an elementary exercise, a notion of how to use the Pen tool is recommended.

1. Open the drawing in Illustrator. To do this, open a new document and place the image (File>Place). A clear image is not necessary because it is going to be completely vectorized.

2. Start to redraw the image that has been opened using the Pen tool. Start with the largest forms in the drawing, such as the torso, legs, head, and arms.

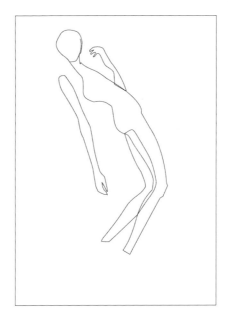

3. One way of seeing what the line looks like is to deactivate the layer where the draft has been placed. It is important that this is not the same as the layer that is being drawn on.

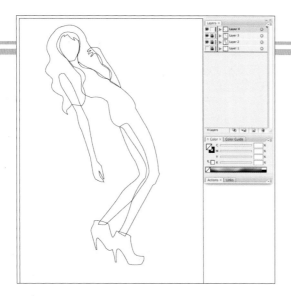 

4. Continue outlining the hair and shoes. It is advisable to lock the layers that are being used in order to prevent you from selecting forms unintentionally.

5. Now the main forms making up the drawing are complete. You should draw each form as a closed area so that it can be colored individually afterwards.

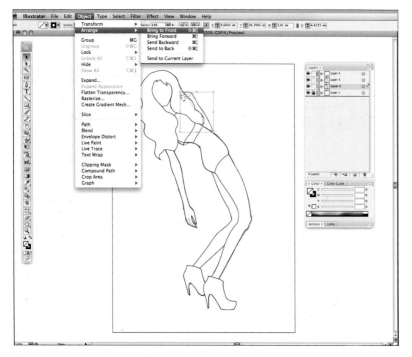

6. The order of elements in the layers – this is very important if the drawing is to look the way it should – is controlled from Object>Arrange on the menu while the order of the layers can be changed simply by moving them up or down on the panel.

7. The face details — eyes, nose, and mouth — are drawn more finely than the outline. This is adjusted in Window>Appearance>Stroke.

8. Draw the hair as a series of wavy lines. Modify their curves by means of the dots that have been drawn in them. The Pen context options enable you to add dots to the line or remove them.

9. Once all of the lines are drawn, check them to see if any dot on the line or its thickness needs altering. Add the last details to complete the drawing.

CREATIVE BRUSH

This exercise shows how to make an illustration with vectors by applying a brush to the line to give it a more personal and artistic touch. This is only a random selection from the wide range of brushes that can be achieved.

1. First, place the freehand draft in the document. Although you can retouch it in Photoshop, this will not be necessary as it will be completely drawn as vectors.

2. Before vectorizing the drawing, double click on the layer it is located on and select the option Dim Images To with a minimum value of 50 percent so that the image is not so dark and the line can be seen.

3. Use the Pen to draw the largest forms in the drawing, which are the jacket and dress in this case.

4. Continue with the arms, legs, and boots. Draw each group of elements on a different layer. When you select one of these, the lines of the elements it contains are shown in different colors.

5. Draw in all of the details of each area little at a time, such as the hat, face, and pleats. Draw with the same thickness as the outline for the time being – this can be changed later.

6. The outline of the hair is made with the Pen, but if you want, you can draw the inside lines with the Pencil tool, which also enables you to fix the dots later.

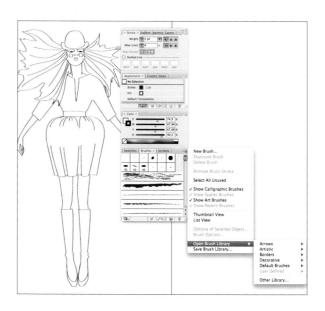

7. Once the entire illustration has been outlined, drop down the Brush menu, select Open Brush Library, and choose the Artistic option.

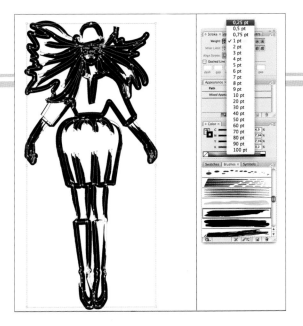

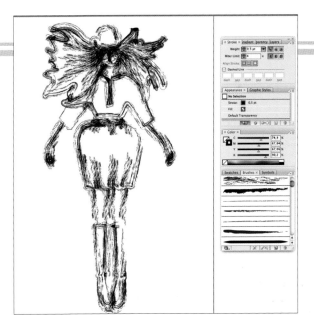

8. You can now try the different brushes and vary their weights with Stroke>Weight on the panel. Depending on the brush, one weight or another will work better.

9. This example shows a brush giving the drawing a more abstract appearance. The brush had a low weight as it is already quite heavy.

10. It is always recommendable that a thinner line be used for the details – such as facial features – because they are represented better in this way.

11 At last, the artistic illustration is finished. Its lines resemble a drawing made in India ink.

LIVE TRACE

This exercise shows how to use the Illustrator Live Trace tool. This tool can become one of the most useful in the program if you know how to work with it. It lets you automatically turn a drawing into vectors, although not all images turn out right if they are vectorized this way. A general recommendation is that the drawing outline is as close as possible to how it would look as vectors and that they should be closed and defined forms (sketches are not very suitable). The result will be of high quality and the use of effects will not be noticeable, which is how it should be.

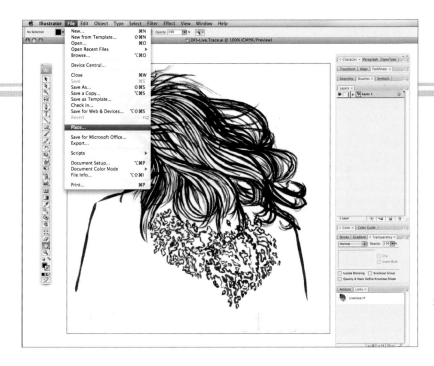

1. The image used here was drawn in India ink. As it is a strongly contrasted image, it will look good with the Live Trace tool. To place it in the document, use File>Place.

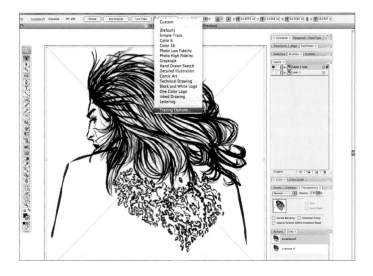

2. Select the image, click on the dropdown menu for Live Trace and select Tracing Options. This enables you to regulate the outline depending on where it is needed most.

2a. The box shows the different tracing options. You can customize your settings or, more simply, chose a predetermined one.

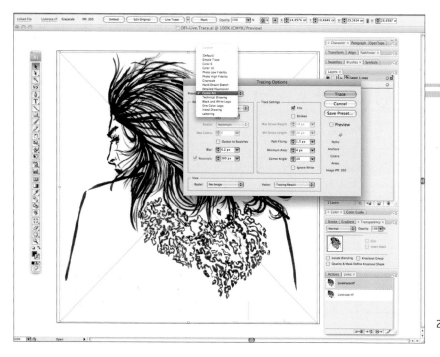

2b. Preset gives the different default options, each allowing you to create a different style of outline.

3. Make your first draft with the Inked Drawing option, as this is the technique used with the original illustration. The problem here is that this setting heavily saturates the black and synthesizes some of the lines incorrectly. This option is therefore not the most suitable.

4. Try Comic Art, which also resembles the style of drawing and gives a better result. The strokes are very faithful to the originals.

5. The image has been vectorized. When doing so, the Ignore White option was selected, meaning that only the black lines were vectorized. Now the vector dots can be used to modify the image.

A close up of each of the images lets you appreciate their quality. The image on the left is the original, which becomes pixelated when enlarged. The image on the right is traced; it maintains the quality of the strokes but you can see that they are not perfect and that they were made with a preset tool.

LINE COLOR

This exercise shows you how to change the color of lines in an illustration and how to delete the background. It introduces Layer Masks and shows you how to use them on a layer. This is a key tool in Photoshop. You need some time to learn how to use it, but once you understand how it works it is very useful because it lets you cover parts of layers without deleting them. It works in grayscale: what is drawn black covers the image, what is in white allows it to be seen, and grays create transparencies. Their intensity depends on the shade of gray.

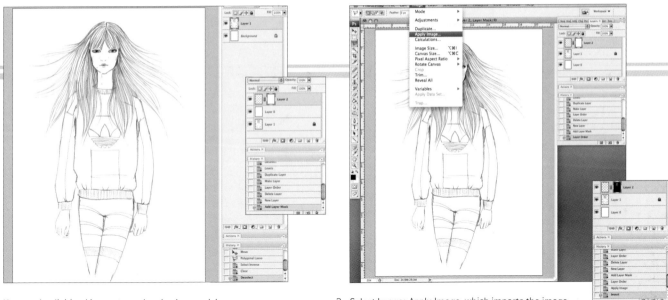

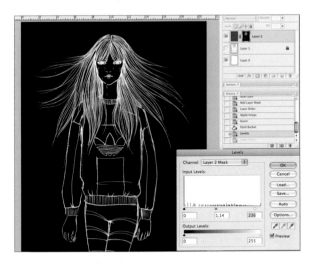

1. You need a digitized image on a clear background. In order to create a Layer Mask, make a new layer. Select the gray square with the white circle in the center at the bottom of the panel. A white rectangle will appear next to the layer.

2. Select Image>Apply Image, which imports the image to the present layer. Invert the image (Ctrl+Shift+I) because you are only going to work with the line. When using Layer Masks, what is visible is in white.

3. To color the line, color the entire mask layer. Even if the layer is completely filled, you can only see the line because it is in the white area of the mask. You can then adjust the layer levels to change the line intensity.

4. By selecting the layer holding the image, you can see what the image looks like with the mask. The white background can be deleted by removing the white layer (Layer 0 in this example), leaving only the blue lines.

BLACK LINES

Fashion illustrations often need to represent black garments. For this to be done well, lines on the fabric need to be lighter. This exercise shows you how to change the color of black lines.

1. Start with the clean drawing and make a copy of the layer to work on, so as to spare the original. It is always a good idea to save the file with a different name so as to keep the originals intact.

2. As with the previous exercise, a Layer Mask is created on a new layer and Apply Image is selected from the Image menu. This will add the visible layers to the mask.

3. To view the mask layer, press Alt and click on it. You can now work on the line.

4. Modify the intensity of the line with Level adjustments. If you select the Preview option, you will immediately see how the adjustments affect the image.

5. Blacken the mask layer completely, given that the general lines are to remain in this color. Then duplicate this layer (the duplicate will be placed below the original). As the lines on the garment are to be gray, use it to color the new layer.

6. Start erasing the parts you want to be gray on the black layer; the gray line on the layer below will start to appear.

7. For more precision when erasing parts of the images, it is recommended that you enlarge the drawing and use a small eraser size so as to have greater control.

8. When the lines of the garment are gray, you can now start to color the image. For the best results, each color should be applied on a different layer (black, flesh tone, yellow, and pink).

The illustration is complete. This is a good example of how it is possible to represent a black garment suitably with plain colors.

CREATIVE LINES

This exercise continues with the momentum of the previous two, and shows you how to modify the lines of an illustration. This creative exercise offers a more complex way of changing a line, and therefore has greater possibilities. The correct use of masks is essential for achieving good results in this exercise.

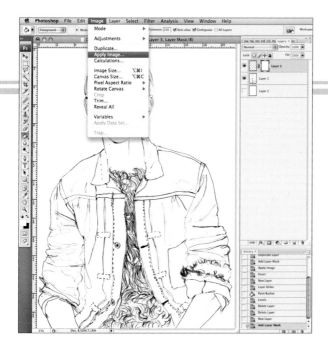

1. Open a clean drawing in Photoshop. Add a new layer and create a mask on it. Then select Image>Apply Image from the menu. Invert the image color (Ctrl+Shift+I).

2. Fix the lines with the image Levels until they are as the way you want them. Then add the color, which is flesh tone in this case.

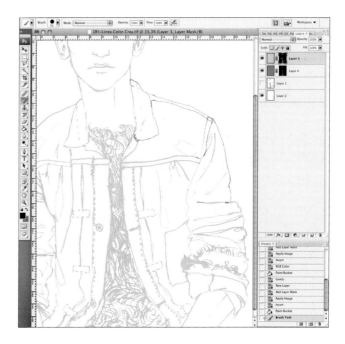

3. Repeat the previous step: add a layer, apply the image, and invert the color. Place this layer below the other.

4. The new layer corresponds to the jacket, so it should be colored blue. When drawing with black on the flesh tone layer, the blue begins to appear. Repeat the process with a layer for the hair (yellow) and the sweater (gray).

5. One way of letting the colors corresponding to each feature show through is to select the area with the Polygonal Lasso.

6. On the masks that do not have this color, fill the selected area with black until only the desired color is seen.

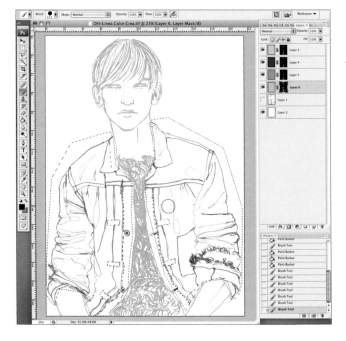

7. Another way of coloring the area is to do it with a brush, which only colors the selected area. This alternative enables you to regulate the values of opacity and the brush flow to create textures.

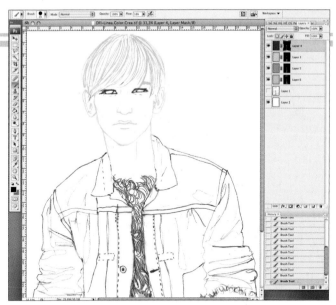

8. Once the jacket, the skin, the eyes, and the hair have been finished, it is now time to bring out the color of the hairy sweater.

9. Once the process is complete, it turns out that the gray of the sweater is not convincing because it should be more striking. Another color will be tried.

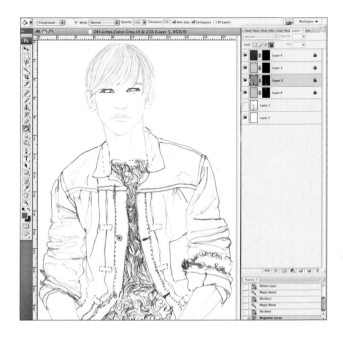

10. To do this, you only need to fill the layer that was previously gray with the new color (fuschia in this case). Since only the sweater mask was modified, only the sweater color will be different.

STAMP FILTER

One of the most popular functions of Photoshop is the Filter option. This exercise shows you how to use it to create an illustration with a more unique and pronounced line. As this is a sketch, only the filters that are used with this kind of work will be shown. You must be very careful with filters because if they are not applied well, the result can be in bad taste.

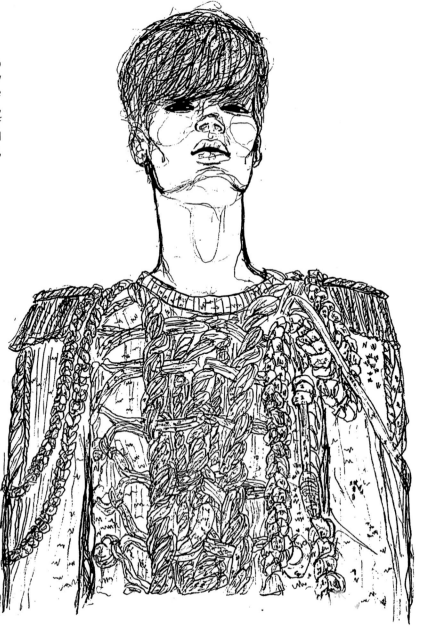

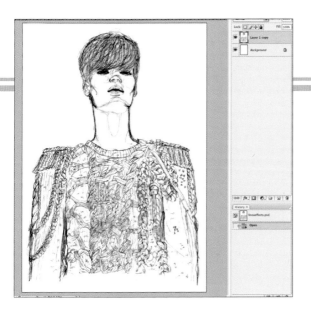

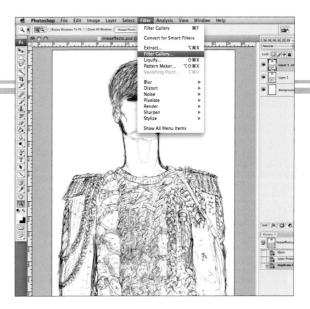

1. The original drawing was cleaned but is still too gray. A filter is needed that provides the image with more contrast and enhances the sweater and its textured knit.

2. Duplicate the image layer and select Filter>Filter Gallery to open a gallery.

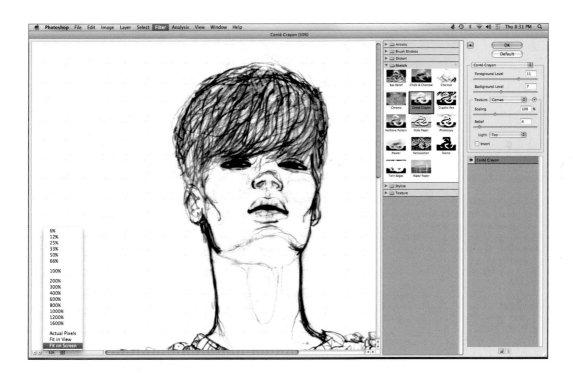

3. The most suitable filters for this particular case are those under Sketch, as they are designed for sketches and line drawings. To see the complete image on the screen, select Fit on Screen from the bottom left.

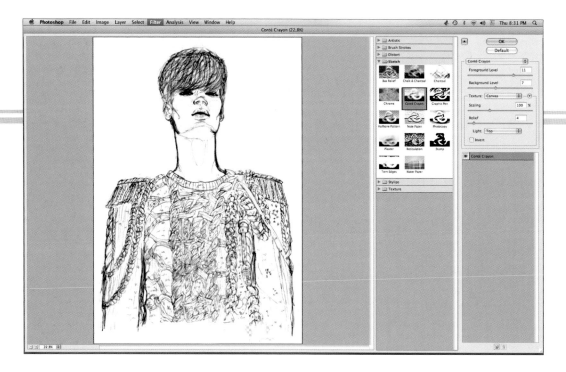

4. An attempt was made with the Conté Crayon, but the result is not too similar to the original. It brings neither contrast nor strength to the image.

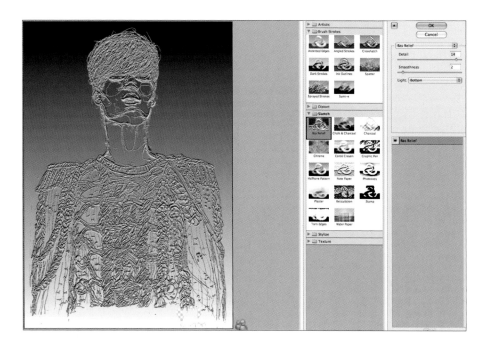

4a. In this example, Bas Relief has been applied to give an effect that is totally different from the original drawing. Although it creates a texture that is visually pleasing, the result is too digital.

4b. A suitable filter was finally found that brought personal-
ity to the sketch. The Stamp filter contrasts the image
and particularly gives clarity and definition to the entire sweater area.

COLOR // COLORING WITH PHOTOSHOP

As with lines. applying color in digital illustration is one of the most important and extensive tools drawing programs offer. Layers are essential for this, and are used to organize the work; each layer is for one color.

This chapter shows you how to apply color generally to forms before the Digital Painting chapter introduces the use of brushes. The first exercise explains the basic way of using plain colors in Photoshop (just like drawing on paper, there are different ways of doing things, and each illustrator has to choose the way that is most comfortable).

1. Make a copy of the original layer of the clean drawing and select Multiply mode. This layer will always
   be on the top so that the lines are never hidden.

2. Use the Magnetic Lasso on the new layer
   to select the areas of skin on the figure.

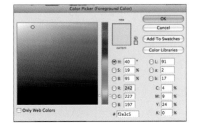

3. Select the tone for the skin with Color
   Picker. You can choose either by clicking
   on the desired color or with percentages.

4. Color the selected area with the Paint Bucket tool. As the
   upper layer is in Multiply mode, which keeps areas in white
   transparent, the color you apply can be seen perfectly.

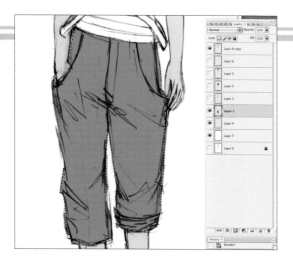

5. Next go on to the pants. As before, select the area with the Magnetic Lasso on a new layer and fill with the Paint Bucket tool.

6. As they are relatively straight lines, areas of the T-shirt can be selected for coloring using the Polygonal Lasso. Then fill the spaces one by one with the Paint Bucket, first with one color, then with the other.

7. Seeing as the vest and shoes are black, select them at the same time (with the Magnetic Lasso, keeping the Shift key pressed) and color them on the same layer.

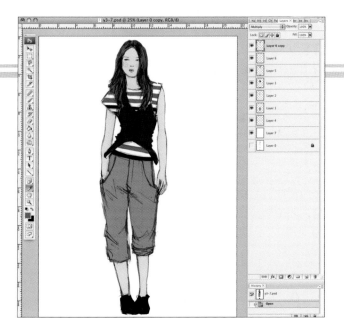

8. Lastly, in the same way, color the hair on one layer and the cheeks and mouth on another. It is important to keep order in the layers you are creating in order to achieve a good result.

One of the advantages of coloring with layers is that it is very easy to change colors later. You only have to go back and color the form you have made from the piece of clothing on its layer. Here the T-shirt, hair, and pants have changed color.

COLORING WITH ILLUSTRATOR

After showing you the Photoshop coloring process, now you will see how it is done in Illustrator. Generally, deciding which program to use depends on how the figure has been drawn. If the drawing was made in freehand, use Photoshop; whereas vectorized drawings should be colored using Illustrator – you cannot use this program to color an image that is not vectorized.

Like Photoshop, Illustrator enables you to change colors simply with one click and offers the option of saving color samples. It also features ranges of preset color swatches that make choosing colors easy.

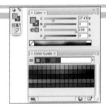

1. Place the sketch (previously cleaned in Photoshop) on a new document (File>Place). It is important to open the Color Guide palettes that allow you to choose from the colors from the list, with the Eyedropper from the CMYK spectrum, or using percentages.

2. First vectorize the skin area with the Pen tool. Make sure the forms can be colored correctly. Then do the dress. To make this easy, work with layers. If you drop down the Layers palette, all of the available strokes will be shown.

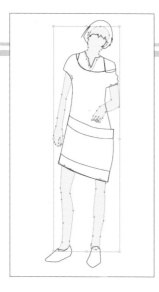

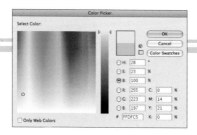

3. Open the Color Picker by double clicking on Fill Color, choose the skin tone, and color the corresponding forms. They must be selected first (by keeping the Shift key pressed it is possible to select more than one form). When a color is accepted, the forms will be filled automatically.

4. Like Photoshop, use the Multiply option to make the original drawing transparent: Transparency>Multiply.

5. It is a good idea to enlarge the image to ensure that everything has been colored. One way of doing this is to select the missing area and clicking on one with the desired color using the Eyedropper. This tool will copy and apply the color.

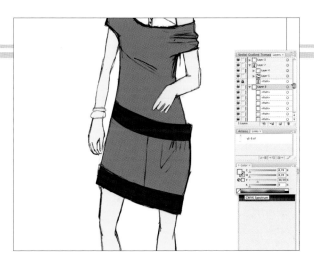

6. Now color the dress. Unlike Photoshop, it is not necessary to place each color on a different layer if they are part of the same feature.

7. Then vectorize the hair and shoes. Initially these have been given the same color, although it can be changed separately later.

9. To finish, vectorize and color the cheeks and lips and do the pupils of the eyes, making sure to they are over a white background.

8. You can try out infinite color combinations until you find the one you want; all you have to do is select the form you want to modify.

COLOR RETOUCHING

Retouching color in Photoshop is one of the most commonly used functions of the program. This exercise uses an image made only with forms in watercolor – letting you have a good idea of using color, which has become a little opaque after scanning. The aim here is to bring back the original colors. The alternative always exists of completely and radically changing the colors and shades.

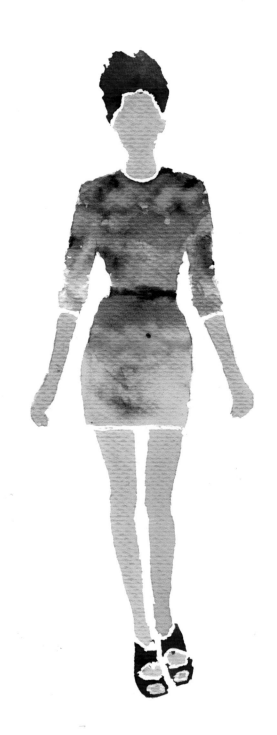

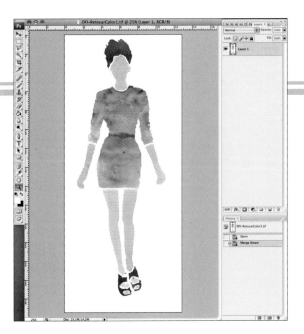

1. Open the image in Photoshop and clean the background so that you can focus only on the color adjustments.

2. Make a new adjustment layer in Levels by clicking on the half-black and half-white circle at the bottom of the Layers palette.

3. Then make another adjustment layer, this time in Selective Color. This will enable you to change the colors freely and give them less or more intensity.

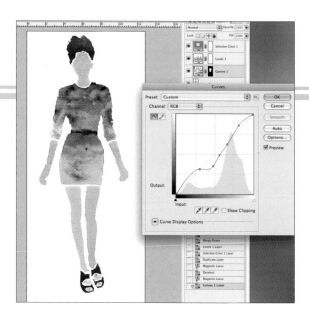

4. The yellows in the initial image are a little opaque so they have to be modified. Choose Yellows in the Selective Color options and adjust the amount of yellow in each color.

5. Make another adjustment layer for Curves, which influences the colors and shades of the image. Moving the curve up or down determines the contrast and brightness of the image. If you add dots to it, you can move with greater detail.

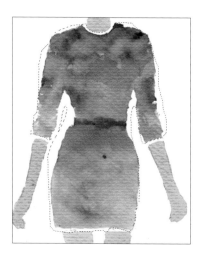

6. Select the dress with the Magnetic Lasso so you can focus exclusively on its color. Now create a mask on the Curves layer. When a selection is made, a mask will automatically be created in the shape of the dress.

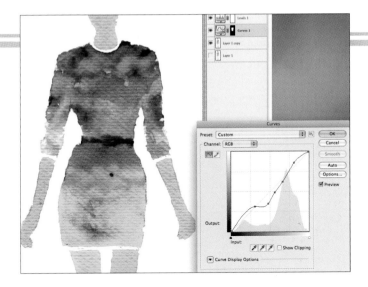

7. Now modify the Curves. The mask protects the rest of the image so that only the adjustments of the dress are affected.

8. The image is then given the desired color and saturation. If you want to continue to retouch the image at a later time, add more adjustment layers.

COLOR GRADING IN ILLUSTRATOR

It is an essential requirement of digital fashion illustration to know how to grade colors as many fabrics are woven or printed with this feature. It is also useful for giving volume to illustrations or for creating backgrounds.

This exercise shows you how to apply linear grading from one color to another in a garment. Once you know how to do this, you can experiment and create color grading on different forms that include a variety of colors.

1. Place the image on a new document. Always keep it as the uppermost layer. Select the image and change the mode to Multiply on the Transparency palette.

2. Start to vectorize the jacket with the Pen tool. Each part (sides, sleeves) is drawn separately given that each linear grading is applied differently to each sector so that the image appears more realistic.

3. Although the pants have no color grading, vectorize it anyway so as to fill it with a plain color. Do the same with the rest of the illustration.

4. Now all of the clothes are vectorized. The lines of each form are in different colors depending on the layer they are on.

5. Select the type of grading you want from the Gradient palette (linear, in this case) followed by the colors you want to use from the Color palette. Here the grading goes from beige to black. Dots have been made in between to vary the grading depending on the spacing between them.

5a. The Gradient tool is used to draw a line on the selected area to modify the angle of color grading and from where to where this is to take place.

6. Go on to the sleeves – separately. These have a different angle from the body and follow the movement of the garment.

7. Once you have finished the grading on each part of the jacket, do the plain colors. Start with the black on hat and pants.

8. Now do the skin tones and facial features. Remember that to color these forms they need to be vectorized first only with fill, not with lines.

9. The figure with color grading is now finished. You need to be patient when using this tool. It is often necessary to make several trials with length and direction before achieving the desired result.

COLOR GRADING IN PHOTOSHOP

Like Illustrator, Photoshop can be used to produce color grading. It offers a number of preset options that can be modified, but you can also start from scratch with the settings you want. This exercise shows a garment with color grading that becomes see-through in the end. This effect can be achieved by adjusting opacity.

1. The illustration has been cleaned and placed on a new layer in Multiply mode. This layer will always remain on top.

2. Start by coloring the skin. You can either use the Brush or Pint Bucket. Just remember to use a new layer for each color.

2a. Unlike Illustrator, plain colors are applied first, at least those that are to be graded.

3. Select the dress with the Magnetic Lasso and create a mask on its layer. Fill it with black and color the dress white so you can see the grading you apply.

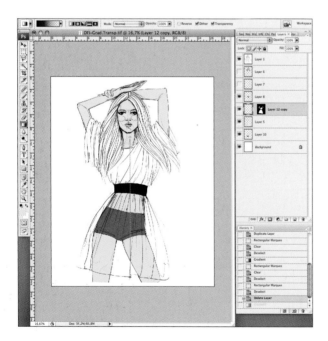

4. Select the Gradient tool and the dress layer, and then try grading. As with Illustrator, the colors and type can be adjusted with the Gradient Editor, which is opened by pressing the Gradient button on the toolbar at the top of the page.

4a. The mask means that the selected gradient is only applied to the dress. As the dress becomes transparent, the model's legs and briefs can be seen through it, giving the illustration a realistic effect.

5. Last of all, the color is added to the hair and makeup applied to the face, eyes, cheeks, and lips. The colors of the face can all be applied to the same layer because no more changes will be made to the image. Now the illustration has grading with transparency.

TRANSPARENCY // TRANSPARENCY IN PHOTOSHOP

See-through fabrics are are commonly recurring feature of fashion, meaning that fashion illustrators need to be able to recreate them in their work.

This exercise shows you a simple way of creating transparent effects by adjusting opacity and layer fills. When working with Photoshop, transparency is quite easy to use and produces satisfactory results.

1. Open and clean the illustration in Photoshop. Set to Multiply mode and color all of the skin on a new layer (select with the Magnetic Lasso and fill with the Brush or Paint Bucket).

2. Select the entire dress and add color, white in this case. As the front of the dress will not be see-through, place it on a different layer.

3. Select the layer with the dress. To create transparency, use Fill on the toolbar and modify its values until you achieve the desired intensity.

4. Once the transparent effect is created, continue to color the larger areas that still need it: the hair and shoes.

5. Finally, add color to the smaller details. Given their size, it is recommendable that you enlarge them and use a basic Brush.

MULTIPLY MODE

This exercise shows you how to create colors with transparency produced with the Mutiply in Blend mode. As its name indicates, this option is useful for multiplying layers as it turns white transparent, as seen in previous exercises. What has not been seen up to now is that the colors of the different layers can be overlapped to create new shades.

1. Paste the illustration onto a new Photoshop document — with a size that enables the entire final drawing to fit — and select Multiply in Blend mode.

2. Color the image. Even if different colors are used, it is interesting to have them all on the one layer.

2a. This image, created with the line and color layers is to be repeated, also by layers.

3. Duplicate the layer containing the lines. Place it to the left and a little higher than the other so that some parts of the dress overlap, allowing the combination of the colors to be seen.

4. Duplicate the color layer of the first silhouette. Fit it to the second silhouette and link them. Select the dress form and fill it with cyan so that the overlapping area of the two dresses becomes navy.

5. Duplicate the layer containing the lines again. To give the image the effect of skipping movement, adjust the distance between the layers and height of each of them.

6. Also duplicate a color layer of the dress and color it
    yellow. It is important to link the line layer with its re-
    spective color (use the Shift key to select both layers
    and right click for the option Link layers) so as to be
    able to move the figures without problems.

This enlargement of the image clearly shows how the
colors are combined when they overlap, without losing opacity when they are on their own. The example
shows that the three basic colors can be combined to
make two new ones: navy blue and green.

CREATIVE TRANSPARENCY

The previous exercises show you how to make basic transparency with two different techniques, which can now be combined to produce creative illustration. At first sight, this image seems somewhat complex to make, but the steps you follow will show how, little by little, you can create an image with greater creative quality using simple tools. The most important thing to make work easy is to keep your layers organized. In this exercise Folders will be used for this purpose.

1. Open the drawing in Photoshop and set it to Multiply Mode. This time a purplish-gray layer will be added as a background – staying under all of the others – to give the illustration a vintage feel.

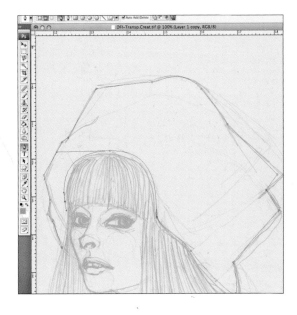

2. Select the hat and coat with the Pen tool, which gives greater stroke precision, for coloring. The Pen should be in Paths mode (the icon of the pen on a square should be selected in the options bar under the menus). To activate the selection, right click and choose Select.

3. Add the flesh tone of the face on one layer and its shading on another. Use a small Brush for the shading. You should finish the central figure before starting with the shapes.

4. Add the details of the face on another layer, also with a Brush. As seen in the Layers palette, create a folder (go to New Group on the dropdown Layers menu). Click and drag the layers you have made so far across to the folder.

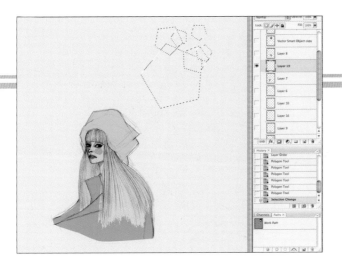

5. Experiment a little with making shapes. Create a new layer, select the Polygon Tool and draw several pentagons (for instance) overlapping one another. Just as you did with the hat outline, activate the selection and apply color with the Paint Bucket. You will see that the overlapping areas remain blank.

6. Now start to draw the figures that resemble the shape of the hat. As with the example, use the Polygon Tool to draw. Fill with the Paint Bucket. Set the layer to Multiply mode.

6a. Continue with the remaining pentagons. Remember to draw each one on a different layer in Multiply mode so that the colors will combine.

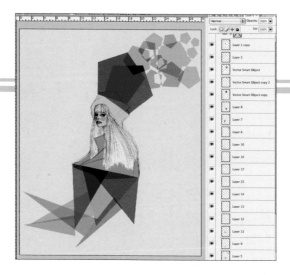

7. Then make the triangles that extend out from the dress with the Polygonal Lasso, the same as the pentagons, each one on a layer in Multiply mode. Open a new folder for the pentagon and triangle layers using the Pass Through option in Blend mode.

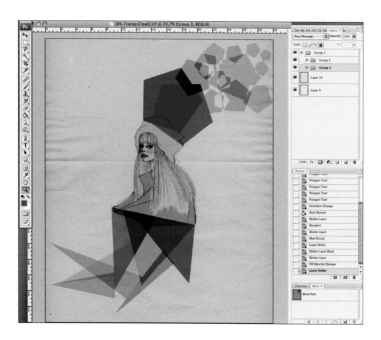

8. To give the illustration a more dynamic effect, add an old paper texture as the background. To do this, drag it from the document it was originally on (it has to have a suitable size and resolution) and place it at the bottom.

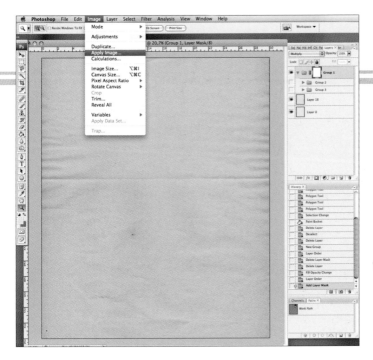

9. In order for the elements to appear integrated with the texture, create a new layer with a mask that is applied to all of the folders. It is important to ensure that when making the mask and selecting Apply Image on the Image menu, only the layers you want to copy onto the mask are active (only the paper texture in this case).

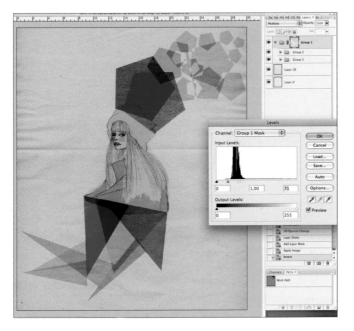

10. Activate all of the layers and invert the mask color (Ctrl+Shift+I). Adjust the values in the levels window until the texture looks good over everything.

COMPOSITION

One of the most difficult things with making an illustration is its composition. This problem is minimized when working digitally because the images can be drawn separately and then assembled. This provides an opportunity for you to adjust the composition until you achieve a satisfactory result.

Here we show how three related illustrations are digitalized and composed on a document until a pleasing layout is achieved before adding color and texture. The Blend layer mode Multiply is used for most of this exercise, first to make the composition process easy, and later for adding texture and color.

1. The three illustrations are drawn on paper. They are originally the same size, but this can later be modified on the computer. When digitizing, keep each of them on a separate document.

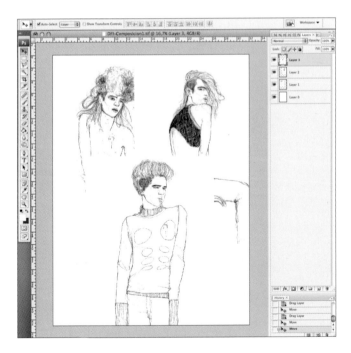

2. Create a new document at 300 dpi and of the size required for the final illustration and drag the three drawings onto it.

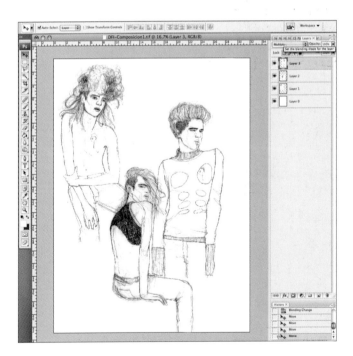

3. All of the layers (except the background) are placed in Blend layer mode Multiply so that the lines of all of the illustrations can be seen.

4. Select the layer and change its size and direction using Edit>Free Transform (Ctrl+T). Press the Shift key when adjusting the figures to maintain their proportion.

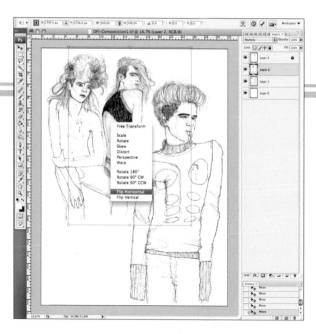

5. Besides modifying the size of this image, horizontal changes are also required: select Free Transform, right click on the mouse and select Flip Horizontal.

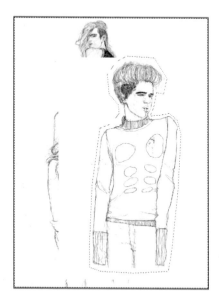

6. Once a pleasing layout is decided on, clean the edges of each figure so that the overlapping parts do not become transparent because the layers will be processed in Blend layer mode Normal.

7. The Polygonal Lasso can be used for large scale elimination of the edges, but to keep the figures well defined, it is recommendable that you enlarge the image and use the small Eraser to delete white areas.

8. When the composition is complete, select the three layers with the figures and use Flatten Image on the Layers menu, which will merge the three layers into a single one.

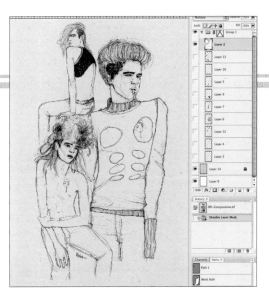

9. Set the new layer to Blend layer mode Multiply. Add a new layer with a background color and a layer with texture over it. Set this to Multiply too, and lower the values of its fill a little.

10. Now color the image starting with the skin. This is done all on one layer set to Blend layer mode Multiply.

11. Continue with the skin shading, which also goes on a layer with Blend layer mode Multiply.

12. Add the hair color – the same for all three figures, seeing as it is the same model in the three drawings– on a new layer, also in Multiply mode.

13. Color the sweater and give it its respective shading. Leave parts around the edges uncolored so as to give movement and feel to the illustration.

14. Color the pants. The two on the left are placed on the same layer, even though they are not the same color, because they are small forms and far apart.

15. Complete this stage of the illustration by doing the final details and shading with basic brushes in different sizes.

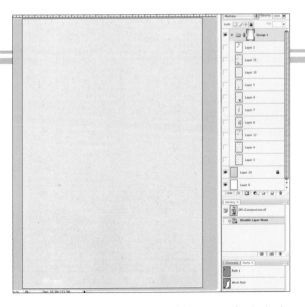

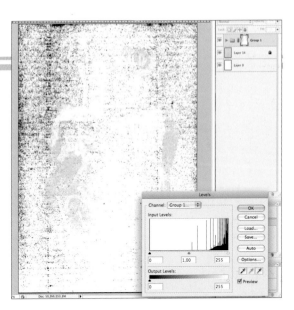

16. Place all of this together in the same folder except for the back-ground texture and color. Deactivate all of the layers inside the folder, create a mask and select Image>Apply Image. Only the texture will be applied to the mask.

17. Invert the mask color (Image>Adjustments>Invert) and adjust the Levels. In order to see what is on the mask, click on it while pressing the Alt key.

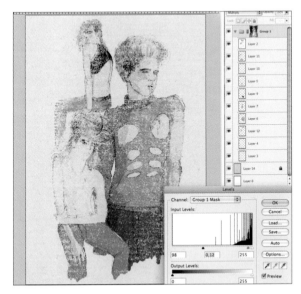

18. Now activate all of the layers to see the effect the texture mask has on them. You can adjust the Levels until you obtain the de-sired effect.

19. The ideal situation is that the texture applied to the Group 1 folder is not too obvious, only giving the impression that the paper is old and worn.

PATTERNED FABRIC //
BASIC PATTERNED FABRICS WITH PHOTOSHOP

Patterned fabrics can be applied in different ways with Photoshop, depending on the result you are trying to achieve in the illustration.

This first exercise starts with the easiest and most basic way to apply a patterned fabric: by scanning a real one. Besides being a very efficient and realistic solution, another benefit with working this way is that when the fabric is digitized, it can keep its form and the colors can be changed as needed. No extreme changes will be made in this case, although with what you have learned in the color retouching exercise, you have the tools and know-how to do those.

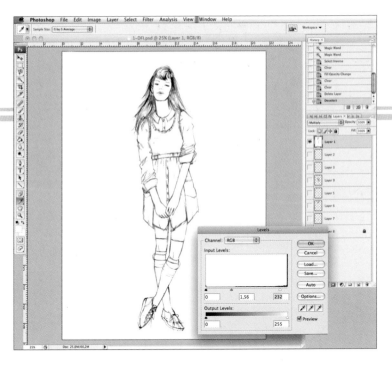

1. Open the cleaned illustration in Photoshop. Select the Blend layer mode Multiply, so that the layer is always on top, and modify the Levels in the Image>Adjustments menu.

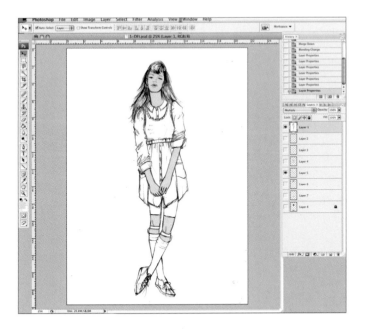

2. Select the skin areas with the Magnetic Lasso and choose the tone you want to use for them in the Color Selector. Apply the color on a new layer.

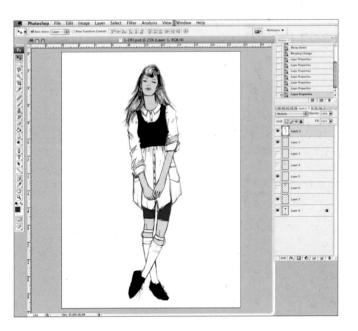

3. Color the vest and shoes on the same layer, seeing they are the same color. The leggings and cheeks go on separate layers.

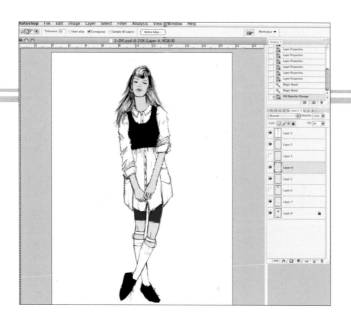

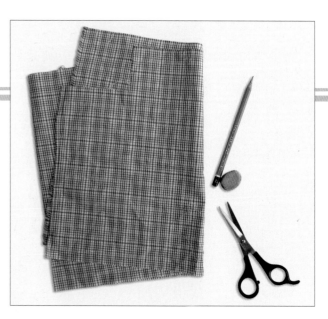

4. Now select the girl's shirt and create a new layer, which is where the patterned fabric will later be applied.

5. This is a photograph of the real patterned fabric. A piece has been cut off so that it can be scanned well and so as not to distort the plaid.

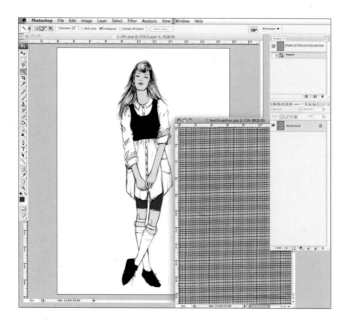

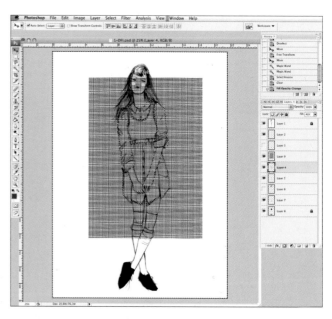

6. In Photoshop open the document with the fabric, which was scanned with the same resolution as the illustration.

7. Drag the fabric over the document with the illustration and place it over the shirt, ensuring it covers the selected area completely.

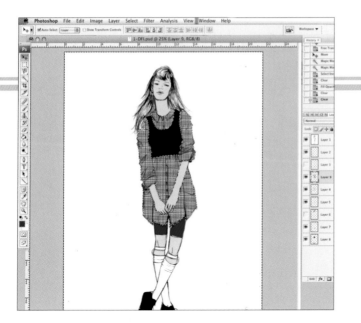

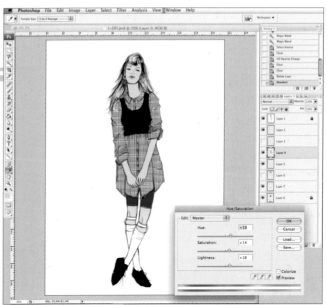

8. With the fabric layer selected, go to Select>Invert in the menu and press the Delete key. This leaves the fabric only in the shirt area.

9. Go to Image>Adjustments>Hue>Saturation in the menu to modify the shade of color. In this case the fabric is given a slightly more greenish tinge than the original.

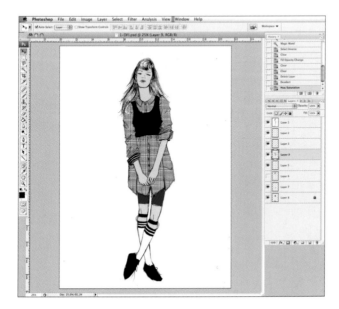

10. Add lines to the socks and sleeve on the shoes and vest layer. Also finish off the lips – on the same layer as the cheeks – and the eyes.

11. The last step is to color the hair. Now you have an illustration incorporating a real fabric in its color scheme, giving it more realism.

CREATIVE DIGITAL PATTERNED FABRIC

This exercise builds on an element already dealt with on a basic level – the plaid fabric used in the previous exercise – to produce a creative illustration.

The method of applying the patterned fabric is the same as previously shown, but the difference is in the type of illustration, which here is more personal and expressive, and emphasis is given to the fabric (featured on a large expanse of this composition for effect).

Additionally, a background made from paper cut-outs has been incorporated, which gives life and volume to the illustration.

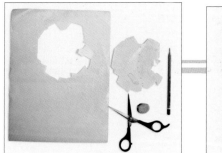

1. Draw the figure on paper. Draw the jacket on a different piece of paper, together with a hand and buttons, and cut them out. By overlaying them onto the drawing, the effect of texture and volume is evident. This effect will be reproduced digitally.

2. Digitize the illustration and the colored paper together. Open them in Photoshop. Create a layer in Multiply mode that only contains the black lines so as to intensify them.

3. Import the patterned fabric on a new layer, also in Multiply mode. Use the Magnetic Lasso to select the outline of the cut-outs, removing the buttons and hand from the selected area (use the Lasso and the Alt key to remove zones from selected areas).

4. Add the background area to be covered with the fabric (use Lasso and Shift key) to the selected area. Be careful not to include the legs.

5. Invert the selection and delete what is now selected so as to only have the fabric in the desired areas.

6. Find an image (or images) from your personal image library that will help to add a personal touch to the illustration; here it is cold and gray. Select the elements with the Polygonal Lasso, simulating the effect of cutting out with scissors.

7. Place each element on a different layer. This enables you to adjust the size of each and with the composition on the whole.

8. To make the sky, make a random selection of pieces of sky with the Polygonal Lasso and copy them to the new composition. Using the same tool and technique keeps unity in the project.

9. Each piece of cloud is imported on a new layer, which is set in Multiply mode to make it translucent and to add depth to the composition.

10. As there are so many cloud layers, select all and go to Layers>Link Layers in the menu (you can also do this by right clicking on the mouse).

11. To make the illustration tidier, all of the cloud layers — now joined — are placed in a new folder.

12. Once the illustration is complete, you can see that the jacket color makes no real contribution as it is distinguishable from the pattern, so the layer is deactivated.

ADJUSTING THE PATTERNED FABRIC IN PHOTOSHOP

In order to give a fabric imported to Photoshop even more realism, it can be adjusted to the form of the garment. Use the Deform option, which enables you to experiment with the three-dimensional nature and volume of the fabric. This works by means of control points you create inside a selected area.

A classic gingham fabric has been chosen for this particular exercise. As it has a linear, horizontal and vertical pattern, it allows you to appreciate clearly the effect and the result produced with this tool.

1. Open the drawing in Photoshop. Clean the image and place the layer in Multiply mode, keeping it at the top throughout the exercise.

2. Use the Magnetic Lasso to select sectors of skin – hand, face, and neck – and fill them on a new layer with the Paint Bucket.

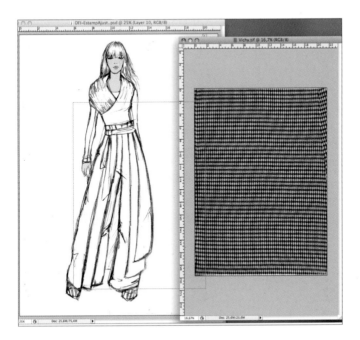

3. Scan the fabric, maintaining the same resolution and format as the illustration. Use the Move tool to drag it to the document containing the illustration.

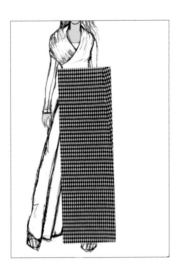

4. As each of the pant legs faces a different direction, their volumes are also different. Work separately with each of them. Starting with the right leg, select an area of fabric to cover it and erase the excess.

5. With the fabric selected, press Ctrl+T to freely transform the selection. Then right-click with the mouse and choose the Deform option. Adjust the points until you achieve the desired volume and direction.

6. Add a mask to the layer in order to adjust the pattern so that only the right pant leg is seen.

7. Import a new area of fabric to cover the left leg. Position the material so that it follows the direction of the fall of the fabric.

8. As with the other leg, use the Deform option and move the points to adjust the direction and volume of the fabric. Then create a mask to cover the area not included in the pants.

9. With the gingham pants now ready, color the rest of the illustration. Color the belt, T-shirt, and shoes on the same layer, as they are all the same color.

10. Color the top in red on one layer, and the lips, and cheeks together on another. Because the color chosen for the face is very bright, adjust the fill of this layer until you achieve a more suitable shade.

11. The last step is to color the hair. You can clearly see that each leg has its correct volume and that the fabric falls in the right direction.

BASIC PATTERNED FABRICS WITH ILLUSTRATOR

The time has come to learn how to apply a patterned fabric to an illustration with Illustrator. The process here is somewhat different than Photoshop, basically because you need to work with vectors instead of images. The Clipping mask is the principal tool. This particular exercise focuses on color, making use of hues in the print for the rest of the illustration to maintain harmony.

1. Place the sketch, previously cleaned in Photoshop, on a new document with File>Place.

2. Trace the area for the fabric, the skirt in this case, with the Pen tool. This produces a vector form that can be filled.

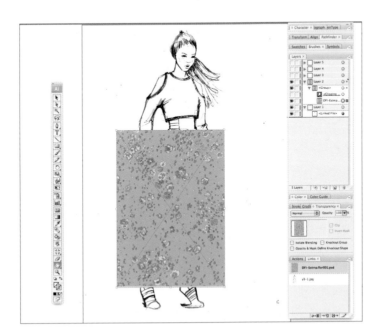

3. Now place the patterned fabric on the document. Once imported to the same layer as the skirt, adjust the motif size (if it is larger than the original, it will be pixelated; just reduce it) and place it over the skirt.

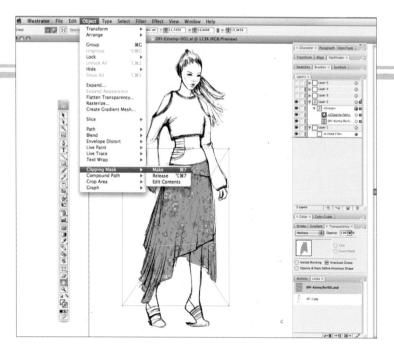

4. Select the skirt and the fabric and choose the option Object>Clipping Mask>Make. For this to work, the vector form of the skirt must be over the fabric.

5. Once the Clipping Mask has been created and selected, choose the Multiply option on the Transparency panel so that the folds of the skirt can be seen from under the mask.

6. Vectorize the rest of the illustration for coloring. Do the areas of skin first. Draw them on a different layer.

7. Go on to the sweater. Black has been chosen for the fill as it is a neutral color and will match the skirt.

8. Draw the complete form of the T-shirt that goes under the sweater and color it yellow. Draw the stripes on the same layer and color them orange.

9. Last of all, color the hair, shoes, and facial details. Here, although they have been placed on different layers, they can be done on one layer as long as the order of the elements is respected.

PATTERNED FABRIC WITH ILLUSTRATOR AND PHOTOSHOP

When making an illustration, there are things you can do that turn out better in Photoshop, and others that work better in Illustrator. Because both programs are from the same company (Adobe), they are designed to be compatible. You can easily work on parts of the illustration separately before joining them as one document.

This exercise is a guide to creating a patterned fabric from a unique motif—to be done in Illustrator, which is more efficient for repeating images—for coloring in Photoshop.

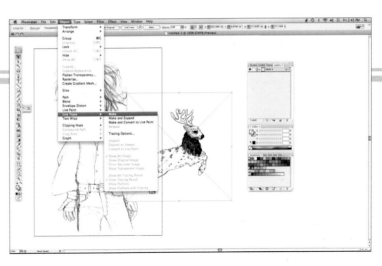

1. Start in Illustrator. Import the image of the figure and the element to be used in the pattern – a deer in this case – on the same document.

2. In order to create a pattern in Illustrator, the motif must first be vectorized. Select the deer and go to Live Trace>Make on the Object menu.

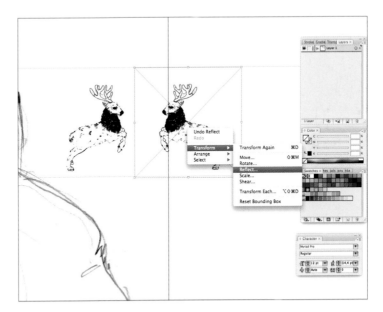

3. Once the drawing is vectorized, adjust the size required for the pattern, in this case so that it is proportionate to the shirt.

4. The pattern is made up of two deer facing each other. You will need to copy the deer, line up the copy in front of the other and paste it. Right click with the mouse and choose Transform>Reflect.

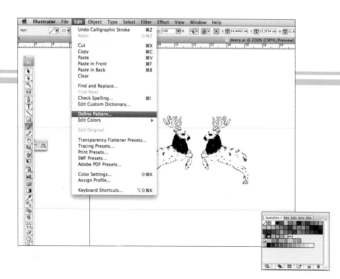

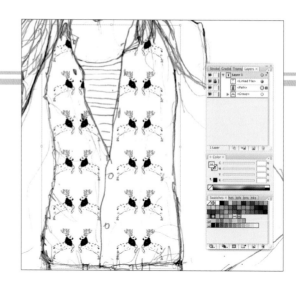

5. Set them at the desired distance apart, group them (Ctrl+G), and choose Define Pattern on the Edit menu. This creates a new pattern, which works like a color to fill outlined forms. It can be found in the Swatches panel.

6. Vectorize the shirt area. Do this without lines. Use the deer motif as fill. If the resulting pattern is not what you expected, you can modify it or create a new one (it is advisable that you only delete the deer when are sure of what you want).

7. Now this patterned fabric is transferred to Photoshop so the rest of the illustration can be colored. To do this, open the figure with this program. Then copy the shirt from the Illustrator document (Ctrl+C) and paste (Ctrl+V) in Photoshop. When you do this, a box will open showing the different paste options. Paste it as a Smart Object.

8. The patterned fabric has been imported from Illustrator. Now it has to be placed over the shirt, which means that the layer containing the figure (now on top) has to be in Multiply mode.

9. Color the rest of the illustration. Leave blank spaces at the edges of the figures to give them character.

10. Because the hair has more movement, trace it with the Pen so that the area is better defined. In the Paths panel, the outline is selected and later filled.

11. The last step is to do the shading on the face, chest, and hands, and to finish off the the edges of the pants so they look like they have been painted.

CREATIVE PATTERNS WITH PHOTOSHOP

Until now, motifs have only been looked at as repetitive patterns – either ready-made or created by the illustrator – to be applied as complete fill for an area. This exercise, however, uses an element as a template, enabling you to reproduce and modify the pattern as you wish. One object can produce thousands of different results.

The element chosen for this illustration is a feather. With only one, you can create a dress of dark feathers, while others float in the air and scatter on the floor.

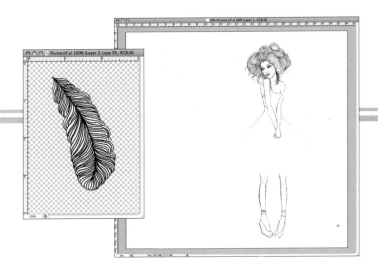

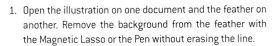

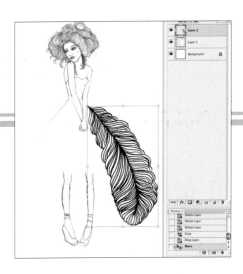

1. Open the illustration on one document and the feather on another. Remove the background from the feather with the Magnetic Lasso or the Pen without erasing the line.

2. Import the document of the girl. When you do this, you will see that the feather is large enough so as not to become pixelated. This is the largest size that it can be used.

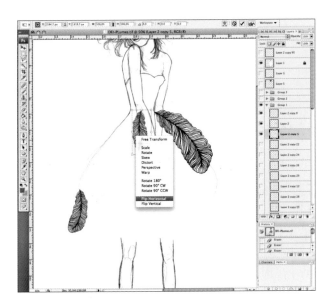

3. Copy the feather layer and use Transform (Ctrl+C) to adjust the size, rotate, and turn over (Flip).

4. One way of doing this more quickly is to select several feathers, go to the Layers palette and right-click to choose Duplicate Layers. This way you will not need to copy them one at a time.

5. Once the desired volume for the lower part of the skirt has been achieved, open a folder and place all of the layers with feathers to make the job easier.

6. The bodice is also covered in feathers, but smaller, so the next set you make have to be that size.

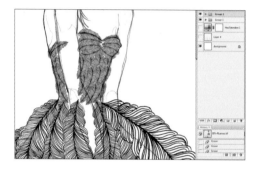

7. Position the feathers to follow the form of the torso and bust, as if they were sewn to the dress. When you have finsihed, create another folder for these layers.

8. In order to clean the feathers from the arms, the layers from each group have to be merged. Right-click over the group and select Merge Group.

9. Use the Polygonal Lasso or the Pen to select the arms and delete this area from both layers (skirt and bodice).

10. Place the feathers that appear to fall. Use feathers of different sizes for a greater effect.

11. Now all of the feathers needed in the illustration are ready: Some come off the bodice and fall to the floor, and others float away, carried by the breeze.

12. Now give the girl color. The shoulders, elbows, and knees have been colored using a medium-sized soft brush.

13. Introduce the desired texture for the background.

14. Because the original color of the texture is very warm and the illustrator had something grayer in mind, a Hue/Saturation Adjustment Layer is added and the saturation is lowered to zero.

PATTERNS WITH SYMBOLS

This type of pattern is similar to the previous exercise. A motif is created for repetition, but not exactly. This time it will be applied as if it were a symbol with the tools Illustrator features for this specific purpose.

In this case, the symbol will be a hair to be used to cover a coat. A choice can be made from the variety offered by the default symbols library that comes with the program.

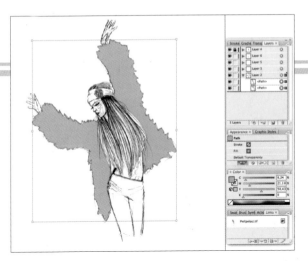

1. The image is previously cleaned in Photoshop and placed on a new Illustrator document. Keep it in Multiply mode over the other layers.

2. Start by vectorizing the hairy coat area. It is important to maintain an irregular outline to intensify the volume of the coat. Color the form without adding a line.

3. Without adding a line, continue tracing and filling the forms requiring flesh tones: the face, hands, and midriff.

4. Then vectorize the form occupied by the hair, which goes over the midriff, and the pants. Both go on the same layer.

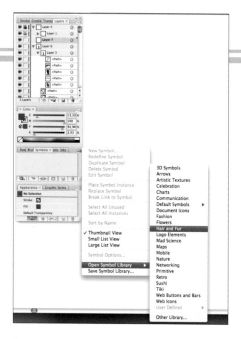

5. Go to the Symbols dropdown menu and choose Open Symbol Library>Hair and Fur.

6. Choose the most suitable hair symbol for the fur type you want to represent. Select the Symbol Sprayer tool from the toolbar and start applying.

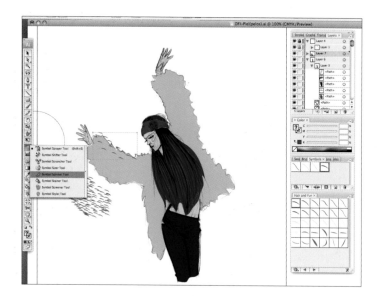

7. The hairs are grouped together as they are sprayed. From the selection you have made, if you want to change the direction of the hairs, use the Symbol Spinner tool.

8. Continue spraying. As the preset distance between each hair is large, use the Symbol Scruncher tool to bring them closer together.

9. To achieve the most suitable color range, the hues have been modified. The hairs on the coat have been rotated a little to give them more movement.

10. A faster way of working is to copy a selection of hairs that have been modified (direction and distance between hairs) and to paste them where they are needed.

11. When the coat is finished, vectorize the facial features and add color to them one at a time. First do the eyes, followed by the cheeks and lips.

12. To finish, feathers are added to the head scarf and the color of the pants has been changed.

TEXTURES // COLOR HALFTONE FILTER

Creating and using textures in digital illustrations is a highly appreciated skill that can bring added value to a project. It is for this reason that it is very useful to know how to apply them correctly.

From among the wide variety of filters available in Photoshop, the Color Halftone filter may be one of the most popular. Generally, it is applied to give an illustration a pop-art feel; this being a look that still has great appeal today. The most interesting thing about this filter is that it lets you see the colors that really bring the forms together.

This exercise shows you how to create a texture with this filter. For this effect to be noticeable, an illustration has been created with strong, well-defined colors.

1. Open the selected drawing (with plenty of color), clean the background and retouch the color if needed until it is ready to have the filter applied to it.

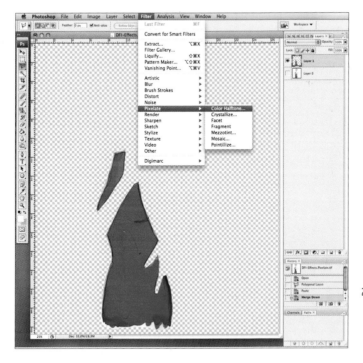

2. Select the outline of the dress with the Magnetic Lasso. Copy (Ctrl+C) and paste it on a new layer. Select Filter>Pixelate>Color Halftone.

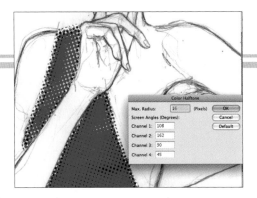

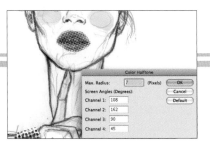

3. In the Color Halftone window, you will see options for modifying the maximum radius of the pixels (Max. Radius) and the filter Channels. In this case, leave it in 16 pixels and keep the channels.

4. Select the lip area with the Magnetic Lasso. Copy it and paste it on a new layer, and apply the same filter as in the last step. This time the maximum radius of the pixels is varied to 7, which creates a smaller dot than in the previous step.

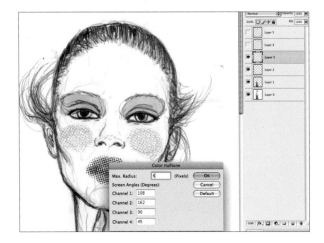

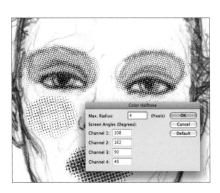

5. Now do the same with the cheeks. This time the maximum radius should be 6.

6. Continue with the eyelids. Again, copy and paste them on a new layer and apply the filter. This time the maximum radius should be 4, the lowest value available.

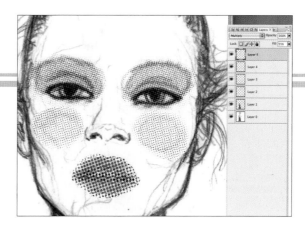

7. Once these effects have been applied, the eyes are not strongly defined. Copy them and paste them on a new layer to be left on top with Blend Layer>Multiply.

7a. The lines of the eyes are intensified without losing the filter effect applied to the lower layers.

7b. When you see the image, you clearly notice the difference in the size of the dots depending on the ratio used and the visual effect this creates (the original color is separated to a degree).

TEXTURE WITH FONTS

Text is used in illustrations to give the message the drawing contains. In this particular case, it will be used this way, but it will also create a background texture that enhances the text on the garment. The star piece of clothing for text is a T-shirt, which is why this illustration makes use of it. The illustrator's favorite city, Berlin, is also featured.

Many fonts come with computer programs. It is also possible to purchase them or download them from specialized websites. They can be manipulated in many ways, the most common being to change their size, color, and direction.

1. Open and clean the illustration in Photoshop. Select the outline and create a Layer Mask to cover the background.

2. The few colors used in the drawing are added now. Select the cheeks and color them on a layer. Do the same with the pants. The lower edge has been applied with a medium brush to create an irregular finish.

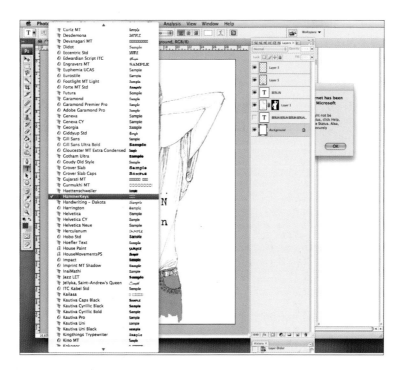

3. Select the horizontal Text Tool and there will be different text options on the tool bar. Choose the font you want to use by clicking in the box for font settings, which will show you the options. In this case, the HammerKeys font has been selected. This was downloaded from the Internet.

4. With the Text Tool still selected, make a rectangle over the T-shirt where the desired text will go. Treat the text like an image when working with it. Create an empty layer over the text and link both layers.

5. The text is manipulated using the Warp option in order to make it appear part of the T-shirt. As it is already an image, use Free Transform (Ctrl+T), right-click and select Warp.

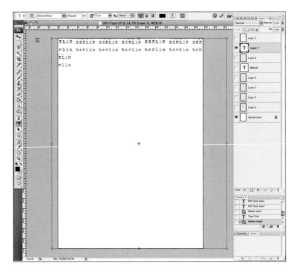

6. Use the control points given with this option and go for the form required for the letters on the T-shirt. Owing to their position, not much is needed, and the warping should not be overdone.

7. To create a background with text, disable all of the layers so you can see only what you are writing. Make the text box bigger than the document so that all of it fits inside.

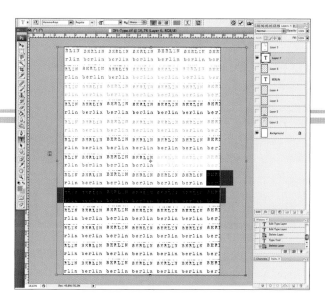

8. Copy and paste words so as to avoid having to write text all over the page. Once this is complete, select areas and add different shades of gray to make the texture more interesting.

9. When the background texture is complete and you are satisfied with the color changes, turn it into an object (create an empty layer and blend it with the text layer).

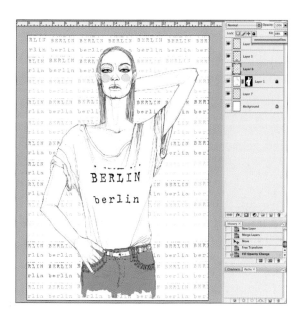

10. As a final touch, soften the Fill of the layer with the font texture so that it appears as a background and does not overwhelm the illustration.

TEXTURED BACKGROUND

The range of textures you can apply to an illustration is an infinite; the texture you add just depends on what you want to convey. For a good result, it is important to experiment with textures and see the effect they give to an illustration before deciding to make it permanent.

Paper textures have been left to one side for this illustration in order to try a new texture – cement. The illustration can be seen clearly over it.

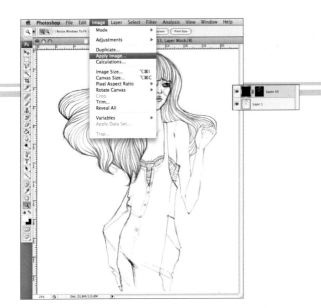

1. Open the illustration in Photoshop. To remove the background, create a new layer with a layer mask. Select Image>Apply Image from the menu and then invert (Ctrl+Shift+I) so that only the lines can be seen. Fill the layer with black.

2. Because the overalls will be black, the lines of the details need to be in a lighter color – gray – to be seen. So copy the layer with the mask and, instead of black, use a gray fill.

3. Select the overalls with the Magnetic Lasso and copy onto a new layer, placed under the ones created using masks. Apply the color fill.

4. Go to the layer with the mask that you previously colored in gray. Trace the stitching on the overalls with white so that the gray lines appear.

5. The lines of the hair need more intensity. Select the hair and paste it onto a layer on top of the illustration. Do this with the Multiply blend mode so that it is not too strong and the line is intensified only a little.

6. Now color the bustier. As the areas are quite small, it is better to do this with a brush. Add each color on a different layer.

7. Use the Magnetic Lasso to select the areas of skin. Choose the desired tone with the Color Picker and fill the selected areas.

8. Select the hair. Add a new layer and fill the shape with the desired color. In this case, we have used dark teal.

9. To give the impression of volume, add streaks in two lighter shades of the same color – each one on a different layer.

10. Complete the details on the illustration before finally adding the cement texture. It is important to ensure that the size and resolution of the background is suitable for importing to the illustration.

11. Drag the texture across and place it under everything. Because it was very gray, the levels have been adjusted using the Image menu to make it warmer and more appropriate for the illustration.

VINTAGE TEXTURE

One of the advantages of digital illustration is the infinite range of possibilities it offers, which enable us to revisit other times and space. This exercise in particular focuses on applying texture. It creates the impression that the illustration was made on very old paper by adding the paper texture and working the edges to appear timeworn. This technique is very popular in digital illustration. It is very difficult to achieve such a good results by other means.

1. Scan the image at 300 dpi and open it in Photoshop. Clean it and place it on a Multiply blending layer.

2. Because the hair is the most extensive area, start by coloring it. Select it with the Magnetic Lasso and color on a new layer. Details such as tips or edges that are not perfect can be fixed with a brush.

3. Select the areas of skin with the Magnetic Lasso and fill them on a new layer.

4. Select the half with the pants and color on a new layer. Do the same with the skirt half. Do the bottom edge and details with a medium brush.

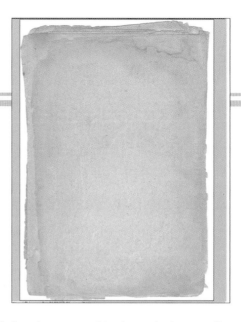

5. Draw the facial features – eyes, cheeks, and lips – on another layer with a fine brush. Place all parts of the figure in a group to keep the illustration organized.

6. Open the texture and drag it onto the document. Remember that the size and resolution of the texture should correspond to those of the illustration. If it is smaller and you try to enlarge it, it will become pixelated and the result will be substandard.

7. Place the texture layer at the bottom and the group with the illustration in Multiply blend mode. Even though it looks good, the full desired effect has not yet been achieved.

8. Add a layer mask to the layer group where you used the same texture as the background. The texture will appear on the illustration, but that is exactly what we are looking for.

9. In order to accentuate the texture, the texture of an old wall is imported and placed over the other layers. Invert its colors (Image>Adjustments>Invert).

10. Duplicate the layer with the new texture. Apply the image from the illustration only (Image>Apply Image) and invert. This will enable only certain details of the inverse texture to be seen, not all of them.

11. Finally, eliminate the layer containing only the inverted texture. You can modify the fill values of the layer with the texture and the mask until the illustration is the way you want it to look.

COLLAGE // BASIC DIGITAL COLLAGE

Unlike traditional collage, digital collage lets you play with images and composition in an infinite number of ways. With the former, there is a limit to the size of the images and how they can be used. There is no Ctrl+Z, so once something has been cut out, it generally must be used in that form on the chosen backing. You cannot retouch the color of the images to blend them or make them contrast, which is something that is easy to do digitally.

This exercise shows you how to create a basic figure where the parts of the body come from different images of models and the fabrics are represented by different textures. The use of layer masks is essential as they enable you to show one part of the image without having to delete it from the document.

1. Sketch the figure you want to make. This will make finding images easier. With your ideas in mind, take your time to find the right material for the design. Look in magazines and on the Internet.

2. Scan the image containing the legs and select them with the Magnetic Lasso. Drag them onto the document with the figure and adjust them to fit the sketch. In this case, the scanned legs were shorter than required, but warping them makes them the right length. Define the outline with a layer mask.

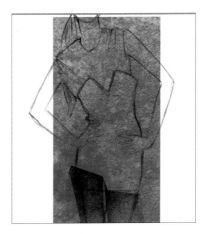

3. Choose an image with textures and bright colors for the dress. Select it with the Rectangular Marquee and drag it onto the figure.

4. To make sure the texture is positioned correctly over the dress, reduce the fill values for the layer.

5. Create a layer mask in the shape of the dress so that the rest of the texture is hidden.

6. The sky from an image that was scanned at 300 dpi will be used for the T-shirt. Select the area with the Rectangular Marquee.

7. Use the Move tool to transfer the texture to the document and place it over the figure's T-shirt.

8. Again, apply a layer mask to cover the part of the texture that is not on the T-shirt area.

9. Scan the image for the left arm. Select the arm with the Magnetic Lasso and drag it onto the document with the figure.

10. Create a layer mask. Use a brush to color the parts not corresponding to the arm on the mask, until only the arm remains.

11. Repeat this process with the image chosen for the right arm. Place these layers over the dress layer.

12. Scan the head image and transfer it onto the document. Adjust the size so that it is proportional. Create a layer mask as before.

13. Finally, add the eyes and a nose from another face to create a unique face.

14. With all of the elements in place in the collage, remove the layer with the sketch to see the finished result. Collage is a means to create visually striking images.

VINTAGE CREATIVE COLLAGE

The most entertaining thing about collages is that you can look in old magazines and books to create compositions reminiscent of those times. This exercise uses images found in magazines from the 1960s and 1970s to create a fashion illustration by means of digital collage. The focus is a garment created from the repetition of pieces from the same image. One of the advantages of digital collage is that you can reuse a "cutout" as often as you like, without there being any alteration to the image.

1. It is important that you take your time to find the right images. If you are looking for old magazines, a flea market might be a good place to start.

2. Once you have chosen the image, scan it and select the outline (it does not have to be perfect) with the Polygonal Lasso.

3. Paste it on a new document and create a layer mask. To cover the part of the cutout you do not want, color it black with a brush.

4. The design includes a mask for the girl's face, so copy a piece of her hair and place it over her eyes. Define its outline with a layer mask.

5. To create the impression that her dress is endless, select wide areas of the dress, copy, and paste them, following the general direction of the folds.

6. A layer mask defines the shape of each piece. Therefore, one way of working more quickly is to duplicate layers that already have a mask rather than creating new ones.

7. Gently turn the copied pieces to be used for the bottom of the dress so that the folds follow the direction of the fabric.

8. Add a texture of old paper as a background to suit the type of illustration you are making. Lower the fill values so that it is not too overwhelming.

9. Scan the image of a sky and incorporate it into the background. Select it with the Magnetic Lasso and drag it onto the figure.

10. Create a layer mask. For a softer effect, apply gray on the mask with a round smoothing brush. Color anything you want to cover in black.

10a. If you want to give the sky depth, duplicate this layer and color the mask again, until it turns out the way you want it.

11. Enable all of the layers. In order to keep everything tidy, place all of the dress layers in a group.

CONTEMPORARY CREATIVE COLLAGE

Of the three exercises in this chapter, this one captures the collage technique the best. It mixes a number of different images, merging them to create an illustration that incorporates a figure in space with the surrealist touch that collages generally have.

In addition to cutouts, flat color – red – is applied to areas to enhance the architectural elements surrounding the figure and to give more depth and perspective to the composition.

1. Look for images in current fashion magazines. This exercise will make use of mostly black and white images.

2. Scan the base image for the figure. Select it with the Polygonal Lasso and transfer it to a new document with the right measurements for the composition. Color the background a winter white color.

3. Create a layer mask. Use a brush to blacken the parts you want to cover on the mask. Also cover the face.

4. Scan an image of eyes. Transfer it onto the document with the illustration, create a layer mask, and carefully cover the background to leave the shape of the hair and eyes. To make this easier, hide the other layers.

5. Now scan the image where the lips are to come from. They will provide a splash of color to the figure. Select the whole face because the nose and cheeks will also be used.

6. Place the image below the layer containing the lips and hair so you can use the previously created space. Create a mask to clean the necessary parts.

7. Use the torso and an arm from another photo. Place it over the layer containing the base figure and make it fit with the head and the raised arm, which will be kept to give the impression that the figure is looking into the distance.

8. Only the legs are left to do before the body is finished. Here they come with a fur skirt and a belt.

9. Place the layer on top so that it covers the skirt and parts of the legs that were previously there. Use a mask to define the figure.

10. To complete the figure, scan the image the hat will come from. This element will add darkness to the composition.

11. This layer is again placed over the others in Multiply blend mode, which saves cleaning the white areas. Sharpen the details with a mask.

12. Complete the composition by adding architectural elements. Black and white images have been chosen in order to blend in with the figure. The positioning of them is a determining factor for framing the figure and creating perspective.

13. The final touch is added by the red slashes. Use a Polygonal Lasso to select the areas, positioning a vanishing point, and then fill them.

DIGITAL PAINTING // PAINTING WITH PHOTOSHOP

The digital painting technique shown in this chapter is the most complex technique in digital illustration. In order to achieve good results using brushes in Photoshop, you need to know how to work with real ones, and you need to master the use of a graphics tablet.

This exercise shows you how to create a realistic image. The original photograph serves as a guide and sets the parameters when painting. This style is even more difficult to paint because you need to have meticulous control over areas and colors of the illustration. You need to be very patient when painting this way and it is recommended that you adjust the graphics palette to make your work as easy as possible.

1. Open and clean the illustration in Photoshop. As a guideline for the different areas for shading, fine lines have been made throughout the sketch, also giving it depth.

2. Use the Magnetic Lasso to select each of the elements in the drawing. Fill them with an intermediate color, each on a different layer. Darker and lighter shades will be added later.

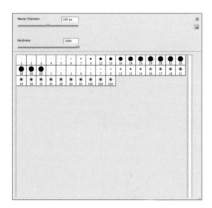

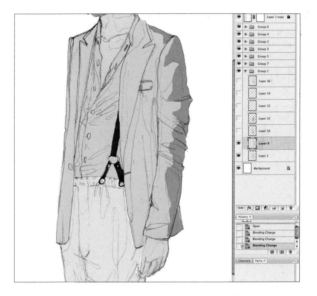

3. This is the Brush Preset Picker window. When you select the Brush tool and click on the brush in the toolbar, this window pops up. You can see the different brush diameters and degrees of hardness.

4. To make things easy, place each layer containing a different color in a different group. Start painting the jacket in a shade that is darker than the base.

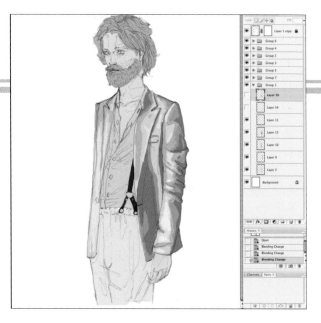

6. Finally, add the lightest and darkest shades to the garment, just like using a paintbrush on canvas. This adds realism and depth to the drawing.

5. Then do the intermediate, darker, and lighter shades. It is recommended you use one layer for each shade so that any mistakes will be easy to erase.

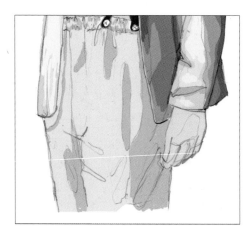

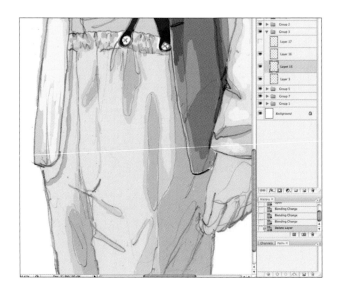

7. Now do the pants. This follows the same process as the one before. Use a shade that is darker than the base color on a new layer. Use the lines of the sketch as a guide.

8. Choose a shade between the two that have already been used to continue painting on a new layer. This will blend with the two and soften the contrast.

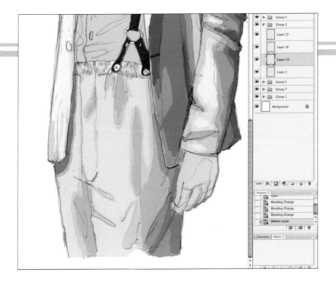

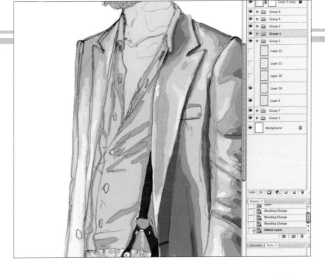

9. Add the darkest shades to the pants. Lighter shades are not required because of the fabric being represented. The darkest shade is the base color.

10. Then do the shirt. Paint it a shade that is darker than the chosen base color. The areas painted in this color can later be painted over in another if required.

11. In order to restrict the chosen shades to the same color, raise or lower the circle in the Color Picker in a straight line.

12. Then do a darker shade. Paint over the areas you colored in the previous step. This leaves areas with color grading for added realism.

13. Color the lightest parts of the shirt to finish it. You can see that these touches give the shirt the required volume.

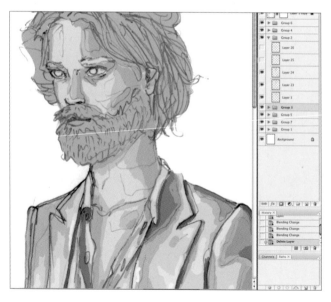

14. Now color the areas of skin. Of all the elements in the illustration, this is the most difficult because it requires great precision and skill in applying color.

15. Paint the darker shades of skin with a brush, including the hands. Remember to adjust the brush diameter for the different areas to increase your precision.

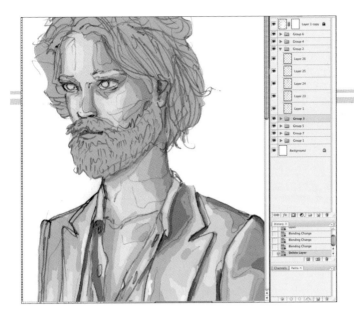

16. Finally, apply a shade that is lighter than the skin and one that is darker than the previously used ones. This produces a realistic effect of volume.

17. The last part is the hair. Start with the intermediate shading following the lines of the sketch, which are guidelines for the direction of the hair and beard.

18. Then add the darker and lighter shades of hair. Paint the eyebrows in a uniform, semi-dark shade.

19. The final details are the eyes. Color them on a new layer: first paint the white part, then the iris in sky blue, and finally the pupil in black.

TRACING WITH PHOTOSHOP

Digital tracing is a basic and effective method, particularly when using a photograph as a reference for an illustration. Working with a graphics tablet, as in this case, offers greater precision than a mouse. However, it needs calibration so that it adjusts to the needs of the specific drawing.

This exercise uses an image of a model as the guideline for an illustrated figure that shares a number of features. Just because you are tracing a photograph does not mean you should make everything the same. It is always good to add a personal touch to your projects and make new and creative images rather than focus on superficial aspects and ease of action.

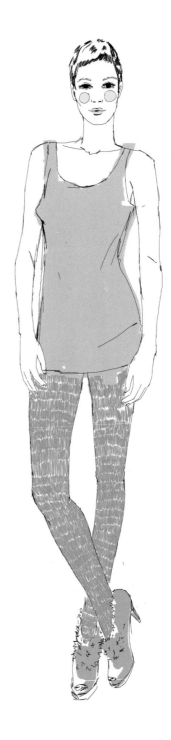

  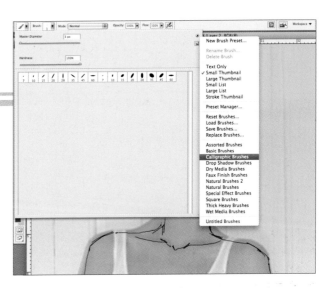

1. Find a photograph with a look similar to what you want to represent. You should start with easy postures to practice drawing with a graphics tablet.

2. Lighten the fill of the photo layer. Seeing this is a fashion model, the length of her legs need stylizing to achieve the right look. Select them with the Rectangular Marquee and stretch them downwards with the Move tool.

3. Open the dropdown brush menu. Select Calligraphic Brushes for a more artistic outline; in this case select the Oval brush at 20 pixels.

 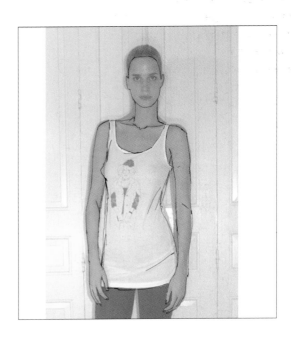

4. Create the outline by drawing it on the graphics tablet. Start with her face and arms. The idea is to achieve an irregular line, similar to freehand drawings on paper.

5. Trace the tank top. As you can see, the image in the photograph is not copied faithfully. Instead, it is stylized as it is being drawn.

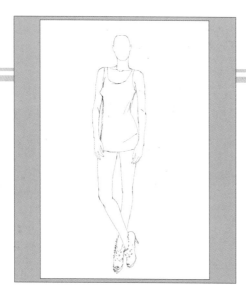

6. When the photo layer is disabled, you can see what the figure's outline looks like. It all goes on one layer.

7. Once the general outline is finished, draw in the facial features on a new layer. Use the eyes, nose, lips, and cheeks as a guide, but use you own style to represent them.

8. Now draw the hair on another layer, this time over the others. Here the style is more illustrative and personal.

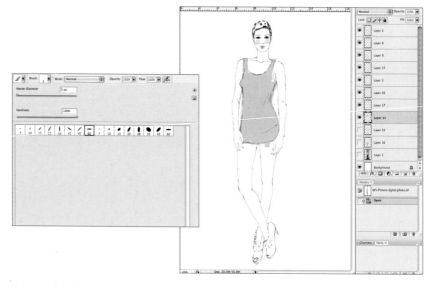

9. Because the tank top is to be colored with a different brush, choose one from the Brush Preset Picker, in this case an Oval brush at 60 pixels. Apply the color on a new layer. You do not have to follow all of the lines and it is good to leave blank spaces in order to let the illustration seem more relaxed.

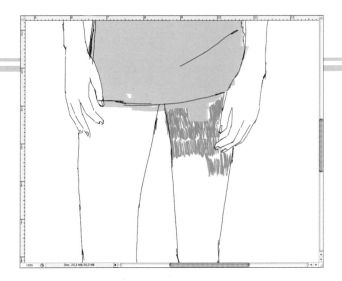

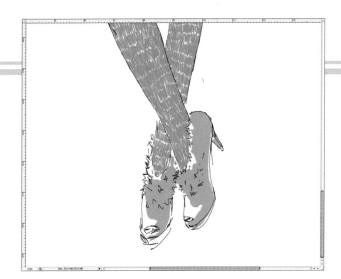

10. Use the previous brush at the same thickness as the line to color the model's leggings. A knit texture is created here.

11. Use a more rounded brush to color the shoes on another layer. Adjust the brush thickness in order to color all of the areas of the figure, such as the tip of the heel.

12. Finally, do the facial details that require color. Erase the line forming the top of the figure's head from the layer containing the outline so that only the hair can be seen.

ILLUSTRATION AND PHOTOGRAPHS

In this exercise, a high-quality photograph is used in combination with an illustration. This is a way of adding an illustrated touch to an already-designed outfit, or, as in this example, a way of creating an illustrated figure to wear a real garment.

The figure is represented in an illustrated fashion with basic features. The use of layer masks is very useful to cover the parts of the real image where digital color is applied. You need to be very careful during this process so that the illustration fits perfectly with the photo.

2. Lower the color levels of the photograph and use a brush to draw the outlines of skin, hair, and face.

1. The photograph for this project should be of high quality, as work will be done at 300 dpi. The most recommendable image format here is TIFF.

3. Create a layer mask on the photograph and carefully blacken the areas that will only be illstrated.

4. Cover the layer mask completely. A small brush has been used with great care to do the garment edges.

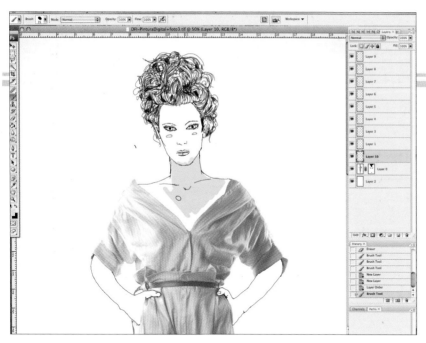

5. Use a large Calligraphic Brush to color the skin on a new layer – this area is larger.

6. The most difficult-to-do areas have been left blank so that they can be colored later with a small-diameter brush.

7. The effect of the illustration-photograph combination can now be appreciated. Finish coloring the arms.

8. The areas containing hands and ankles require a smaller brush as they are more detailed and reduced.

9. Use basic brushes for the hair – a large one for larger areas and a smaller one for shaping and for some of the details.

10. Color the facial features – eyes, cheeks, and lips – last of all. Do the eye makeup with a soft brush to give the effect of eye shadow.

TRACING WITH ILLUSTRATOR

This exercise explains how to use vectors to create a realistic illustration from a photograph. The difficulty lies in mastering Illustrator. If you are experienced with this program, it will be a long but simple process. However, it will be a complex exercise if you are new to it.

The idea here is to copy the photograph as faithfully as possible, so special care should be given to the strokes made. The Pathfinder tool, which serves especially to create new shapes from the superimposed objects, is introduced in this exercise.

1. Set the photograph on a new document and soften the image by up to 30 percent so you can see clearly what you are tracing. Start to trace the outline of the face with the Pen.

2. Now do the arms and neck. Outline these as a single element. They should be closed spaces so that they can be colored properly.

3. Patiently and carefully, trace the outline of the hair with the Pen. Try to keep its form and volume.

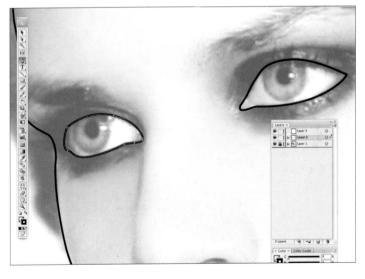

4. Once the large shapes are done, start with the details. The eyes must be vectorized perfectly so that the perspective is correct and so that the model is not gazing into space.

5. To achieve the exact shape of the iris, first draw a figure that follows its outline faithfully in the eye. It does not matter if it goes beyond the line of the eye.

6. Copy the eye shape and paste it in front (Ctrl+F). Select this element and the iris in the Pathfinder window. Select the Intersect Shape Areas option and press Expand.

7. Now draw the eyelids. Use the same procedure to do the other eye and outline the eyebrows.

8. Now it is time to do the nose and mouth. These features determine the look of the illustration, so they must be traced as well as possible. Trace the outline of the shading under the jaw line.

9. Trace the model's earrings, hair elastic, and nails, and the straps of her top. Also trace the lines that give her lips volume.

10. Add color. As you fill the spaces, erase the black line so that only the color is left (the effect of eyeliner is created by coloring with black).

11. One way of choosing color for the figure is to take it from the photograph directly using the Eyedropper tool.

12. Apply color to the hair. The outline of the hands should end up over the hair. If this is not the case, invert the order of the layers.

13. Color the arms, the hair elastic, and the straps. The image is very two-dimensional at present, so more details need to be added.

14. To obtain a real notion of your progress with the illustration and so as not to see the photograph, color the background uniformly.

15. Give the hair volume and movement by creating shapes similar to lighter streaks that follow the hair's natural direction.

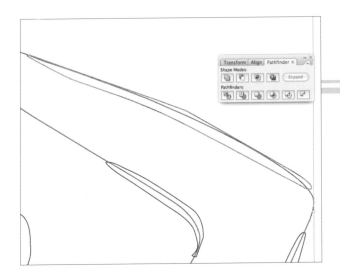

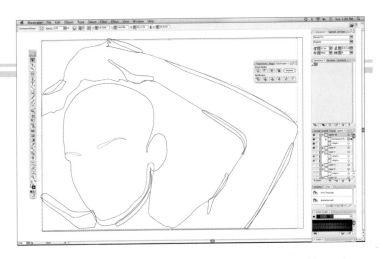

16. You need to give the arms the impression of volume, so create shading. To draw the shapes, use Pathfinder>Intersect Shape Areas, as you did when drawing the iris.

17. First draw all of the shapes and then start to intersect them. Remember to copy and paste the arms in front as many times as there are shaded areas.

18. Coloring the shaded areas of the arms and hands immediately adds a three-dimensional quality to the illustration.

19. As a last step, add shading to the finer details, such as the eyes, cheeks, and lips, and a large shaded area on the figure's left shoulder.

MIXED TECHNIQUES // WATERCOLOR

When working with watercolors, it is impossible to correct what you have done. If you are not happy with the result, the only solution is to do the illustration all over again. This is why it is very useful to be able to clean and modify your illustration, and to join it to another watercolor image.

This exercise deals with the figure and the background separately, later combining them in Photoshop. The figure was created using masking fluid applied around it to preserve the watercolor paint. This method leaves a rough outline around the figure. Digital technology is then used to clean it and join it to the background.

1. The first step is to create the watercolor images – the figure on one sheet of paper and the background on the other. The colors you use are not very important because they can be changed later.

2. Scan both images at 300 dpi, TIFF format, and open them in Photoshop. Clean the figure and erase its background.

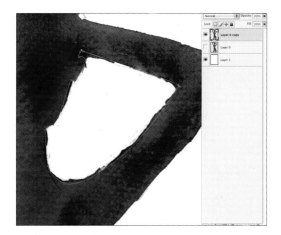

3. Use the Pen tool to define its outline. This tool enables you to redraw the outline with great precision.

4. The outline becomes a selection. Color them black on a layer mask to cover these areas of the illustration.

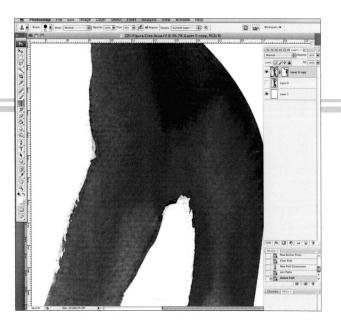

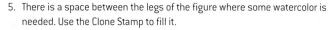

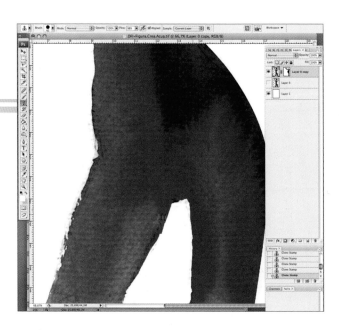

5. There is a space between the legs of the figure where some watercolor is needed. Use the Clone Stamp to fill it.

5a. To use this tool, place the cursor over the area you want to clone and left-click with the Alt key pressed. Now color the desired area as if you were using a brush.

6. The outline of the figure is now completely cleaned. The difference between the initial figure and this one is very evident.

7. To merge the image with its mask, select and click on the Recycle Bin icon. A warning will appear requesting whether you wish to apply the mask before deleting it. Click on Apply.

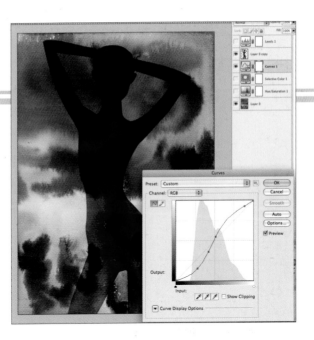

8. Transfer the figure onto the document with the background. Set the layer with the figure to Multiply blend mode so that you can see the texture of the background over the image.

9. Experiment with the background tones. To do this, create an adjustment layer with Curves, where the values can be modified.

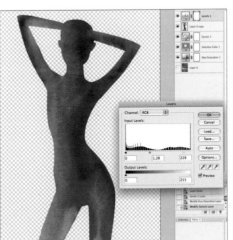

10. To enhance the colors, create an adjustment layer with Selective Correction, where the percentages can be modified, followed by a Hue/Saturation layer, where the color saturation can be increased.

11. Create a Levels adjustment layer over the figure layer, and modify the levels until the figure blends harmoniously with the background.

12. The composition is now finished. Both images have been modified to blend perfectly and you cannot tell that one image is superimposed over another.

WORKING WITH SPLOTCHES

Fashion illustration is always looking for creative ways to represent fabrics and garments. This exercise is a good example of this; a watercolor splotch will be the means to provide a dress with color. The result of the illustration would be almost impossible to achieve on paper if it were made over an original, as there are drops where an arm is located and ones that start at the top of the page. The illustration is separated into two parts: the first is where the lines are drawn, and the other is the watercolor splotch. These will later be combined in Photoshop.

1. First, sketch the figure on one sheet of paper. Then make a watercolor splotch that roughly follows the silhouette of the dress so that both forms will fit well.

2. Scan both images (do the figure in grayscale) at 300 dpi and in TIFF format. Open them in Photoshop.

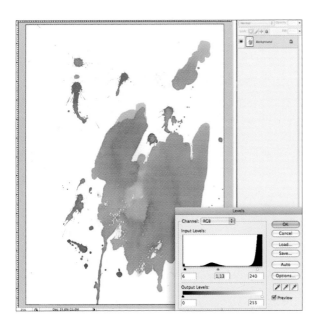

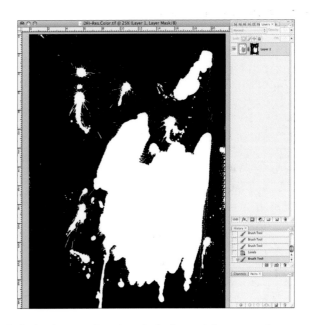

3. Adjust the Levels of the color splotch in order to enhance the color. Clean the background a little.

4. Apply a layer mask to clean the background. You can see the mask by left-clicking on the mouse while pressing Alt.

5. Once the background is clean, merge the image of the splotch with its mask by selecting it and clicking on the Recycle Bin icon. A warning will appear requesting whether you wish to apply the mask before deleting it. Click on Apply.

6. Transfer the splotch to a new document. Do the same with the sketch. Set the latter in Multiply blend mode.

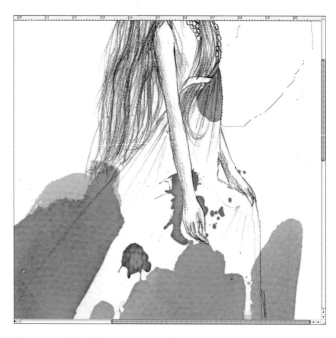

7. Position the splotch exactly where you want it and create a mask on its layer that covers the parts of the watercolor you do not want, such as where the hand is.

8. Clean away the splotch at the top of the dress. Color the selected area on the mask in a black that is not 100 percent so that the white background appears and the splotch becomes somewhat translucent.

9. Do the lower part of the dress. Use the Pen tool for greater precision when selecting the part of the splotch to erase.

10. The pencil lines will appear a little soft. Adjust Levels to intensify them, in addition to whitening the background a little more.

11. Leave the lower end with the natural dripped effect, which gives the illustration a touch of abstract and adds to its creativity.

DRAWING AND PHOTOGRAPHS

You have already seen other ways of modifying a photograph with illustrations, but now it time to see one of the easiest and most popular ways of doing this: adding a drawing onto a photograph. The recommended way of doing this is to print out the photograph and, working over a light table, place a sheet of paper over it and create the desired illustration, which will have the right proportion for the image to be retouched.

For this particular image, a photo was chosen to match the illustration, inspired in Martin Margiela's 20th collection featuring twins walking down the runway together.

1. First, draw the figures on paper and scan them. Because they both have the same body, you only need to draw one entirely and the hair of the other. The second body can be assembled using Photoshop.

2. Select the hair you want to use in the montage and transfer it onto a new document where the body has already been pasted. Position the hair in its approximate place.

3. Flip the figure horizontally. Erase the original hair and clean the outline of the new hair. Once you have your desired image, merge the layers.

Now that you have both figures and the photograph, the process can now commence.

4. Create a new document a little larger than the photo, leaving a white edge. Transfer the three images to this document, although you have to disable the figure layers in order to ensure the photo is acceptable.

5. Enable the layer of one of the figures and position it so that the string of hair she is holding coincides with the unicorn. As the sketch was over the photograph, there should be little need for adjustment.

6. Enable the layer of the other figure and put her in position. It is important to make sure they are the same size. You can do this with the page guideline.

7. Open a new layer. Use the Magnetic Lasso to select the shirt worn by the girl on the left and color it white.

8. Because the white does not result in a creative effect, try different layer blend modes. The choice in the end is Difference, which softens the color contrast produced by the layer.

9. Repeat the last step with the other figure. Difference blend mode makes the white fill take on a color inverse to the background image.

10. The photograph with a fashion illustration is now complete. This type of blending generally works well and is fast and easy to do.

VECTOR DRAWING AND PHOTOGRAPHS

This exercise shows how to modify a fashion photograph by adding vector drawings. In this particular case, the added element was related to the chosen image, set in a harbor. The water scene led to the idea of marine animals and Japanese octopus woodcuts. The images found served as inspiration for the depiction of tentacles wrapped around the figure of the girl. These were drawn over a light table, allowing the background image to be seen when designing the tentacles and the tentacles to be correctly positioned.

1. Scan the India ink drawing of the tentacles and the Polaroid photograph that is the base of the illustration.

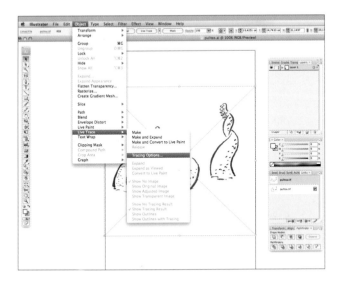

2. Open the drawing in Illustrator. Use Object>Live Trace>Tracing Options to vectorize it so that its lines can be freely modified.

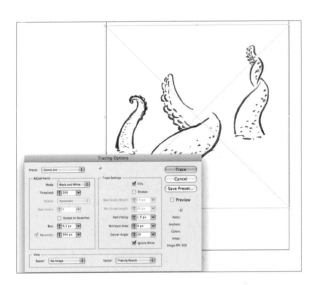

3. Choose the preset adjustment Comic Art and mark the option Ignore White (you only want to trace the line).

3a. The drawing, very faithful to the original, is done as a vector outline. As it is in 100 percent black, it appears much more intense than the scanned image.

4. Import the photograph to the document and place it in a layer below the tentacle layer. Adjust the position of the tentacles, particularly the one wrapped around the girl.

5. Make vector drawings of the tentacle shapes that will be colored orange. They do not need to be perfect, as the black line will go on top of the shapes.

6. Choose the desired shade of orange – from the sample or with the Color Picker – and color the first tentacle. Use the Eyedropper to fill the other tentacles.

7. Group the tentacle coloring with their lines. This way they can be moved together to fit the photo correctly, in case any more adjustments are needed.

8. Finally, color the insides of the tentacles a very soft orange and group them with the other elements, in case you need to move them.

PENCIL AND WOOD TEXTURE

The ability to apply digital textures to an illustration enables you to create a visual effect that makes it appear as if you were working in a different medium.

This exercise makes particular use of one if the most popular mediums for artists: wood. Illustrations made on this material are very beautiful and have a very fine finish. However, this result involves a lot of work for the illustrator because, to start with, the work is restricted to materials that are specifically for wood.

The following shows you how to achieve an illustration with the same quality as one done on wood, but in a much simpler way.

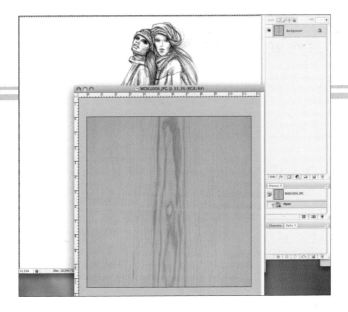

1. Open the elements to be included in the illustration with Photoshop. The wood texture in this case was downloaded from Internet after previously verifying the maximum size that could be used.

2. Copy both elements onto a new document. The figures are on the top layer and in Multiply layer blend mode.

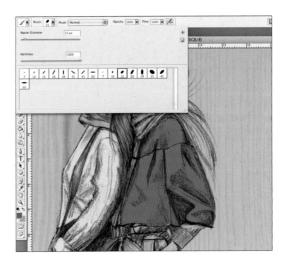

3. Color the figures with a Brush to achieve a more delicate result. Open Calligraphic Brushes and select the Oval at 15 pixels.

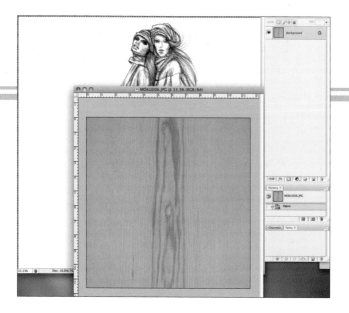

4. Color each garment on a different layer. Start with the largest ones, such as the pants, jacket, and shirt. You should regulate the brush size to adapt it to each area.

5. Color the scarves and shoes. To maintain a harmonious color scheme, try using each color on more than one item (the same green is used on the shoes and scarf, and the same gray is on the pants and scarf in the other figure).

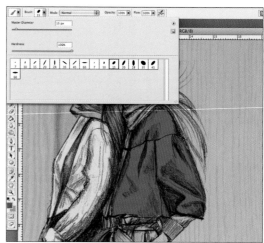

6. Now color the face and hair details. To keep a sense of movement for the blond figure, it is not necessary to stay within the pencil lines. The brush strokes should be random.

7. Once the figures are colored, you can decide to add a touch of color and energy to the illustration. This figure was created with the Pen tool on a layer in Multiply layer blend mode so that it merges with the wood texture of the background.

8. Reproduce this shape on another layer and color the lower area in green. The layer is also set in Multiply and shifted a little downward so that there is a color overlap where both layers intersect.

PENCIL AND PHOTOGRAPHS

It is often thought that good illustrations take a long time to create, but this is not always true. Working in a world where things move quickly, you need the ability and techniques to create quality illustrations in little time, which is the great thing about digital illustration.

This last exercise attempts to create a fun image without being laborious. Again, it is based on a pencil sketch. This is later mixed with images downloaded from the Internet, which, as you have seen throughout this book, is an important resource for illustrators.

1. Open the sketched illustration in Photoshop. Sometimes it is a good idea to sharpen the line as a little can be lost when scanning, but be careful not to change the shade of gray.

2. Choose the Ellipse tool and make perfect circles on a new layer (keeping the Shift key pressed) around and over the girl.

3. In the Paths panel, right-click over Work Strokes and choose Select to enable the circles. This will enable you to fill them. When you do this, you will see that the intersections have no color.

4. In order to paint the dress, it is recommendable to disable the layer with the circles. Select the dress with the Magnetic Lasso and fill it with color. Use a small brush for the finer details.

5. Enable the layer with the circles again and reduce the color saturation by about 50 percent to create a color effect where the circles overlap the dress.

6. Open the wolf image and select its outline. To avoid a very sharp edge, go to Select>Refine Edge and choose the most suitable option from the menu. Here, the Feather option was used to modify it.

7. Transfer the wolf onto the document with the girl. You can see that the soft edge was a good choice and bends in well with the image.

8. To completely integrate the wolf with the illustration, select the Overlay layer blend mode, which colors the wolf in the same hues as the circle.

9. Select the other chosen wolf and modify the edge of the selected area. This time the Radius value is modified to create a softer effect.

10. Transfer it to the illustration document and position it in its corresponding circle. Set this new layer to Overlay blend mode, too.